COLORING BOOKS
FOR GROWN-UPS

Mermaids, Fairies & Fantasy

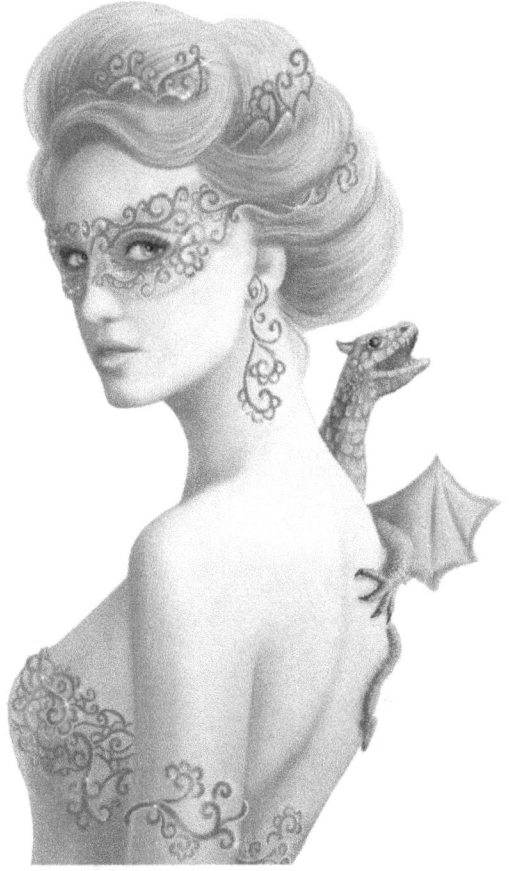

Interior and cover design by Cheryl Casey.
© 2015 Cheryl Casey. All rights reserved.
ISBN-13: 978-1519101266
ISBN-10: 1519101260

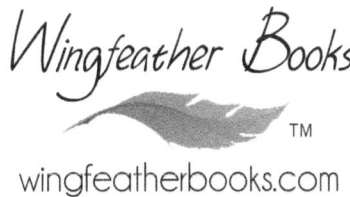

Wingfeather Books
™
wingfeatherbooks.com

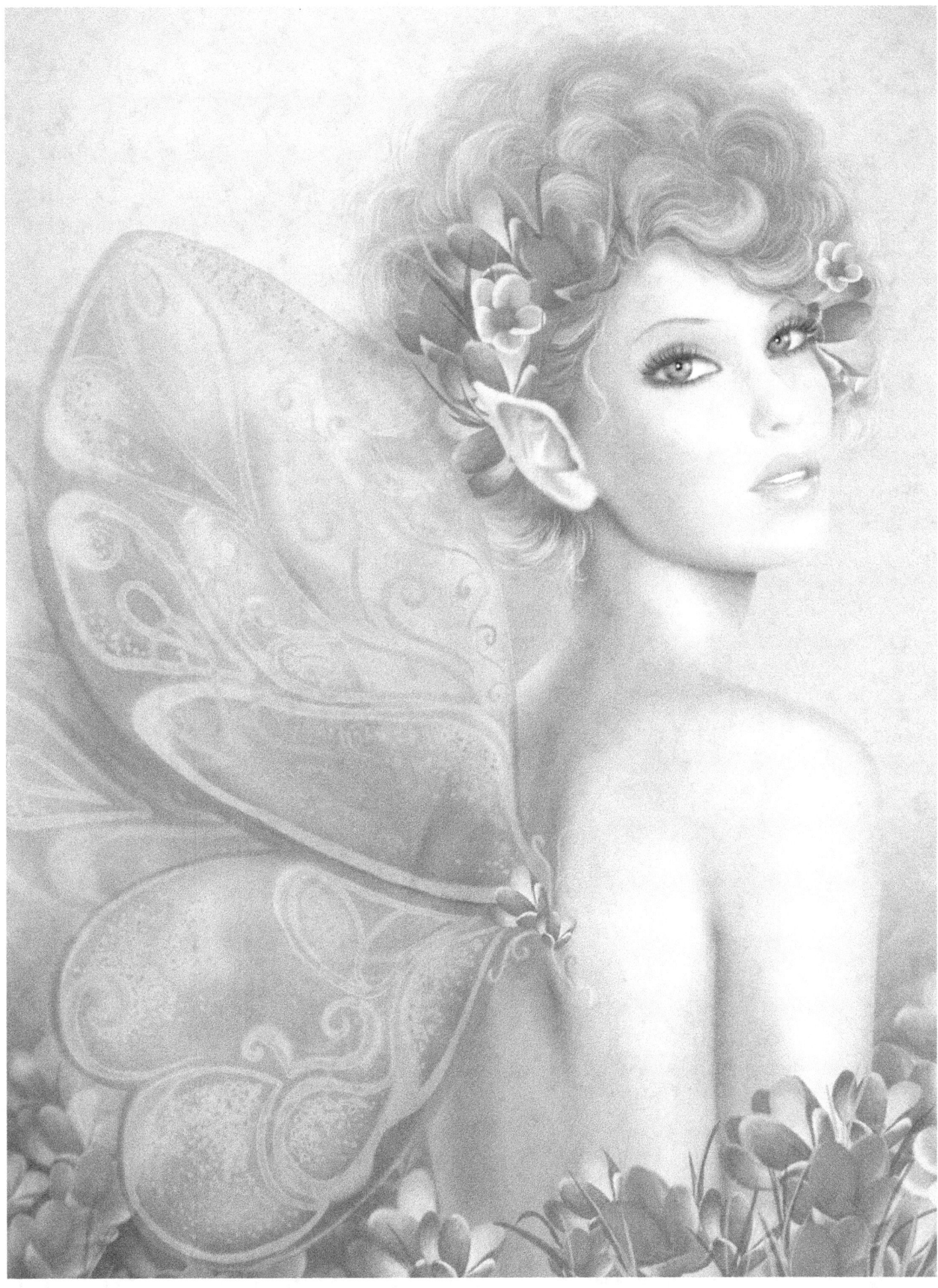

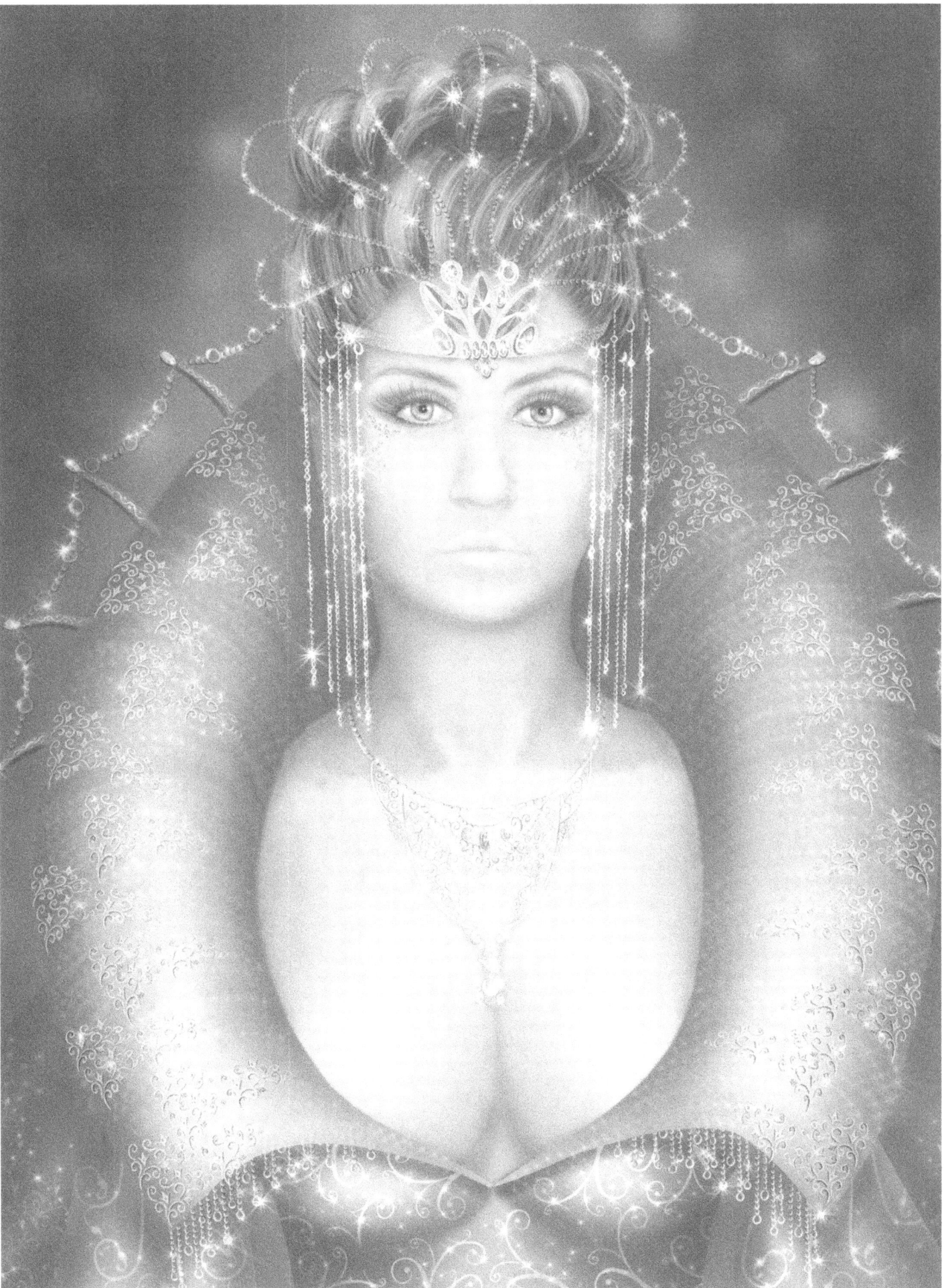

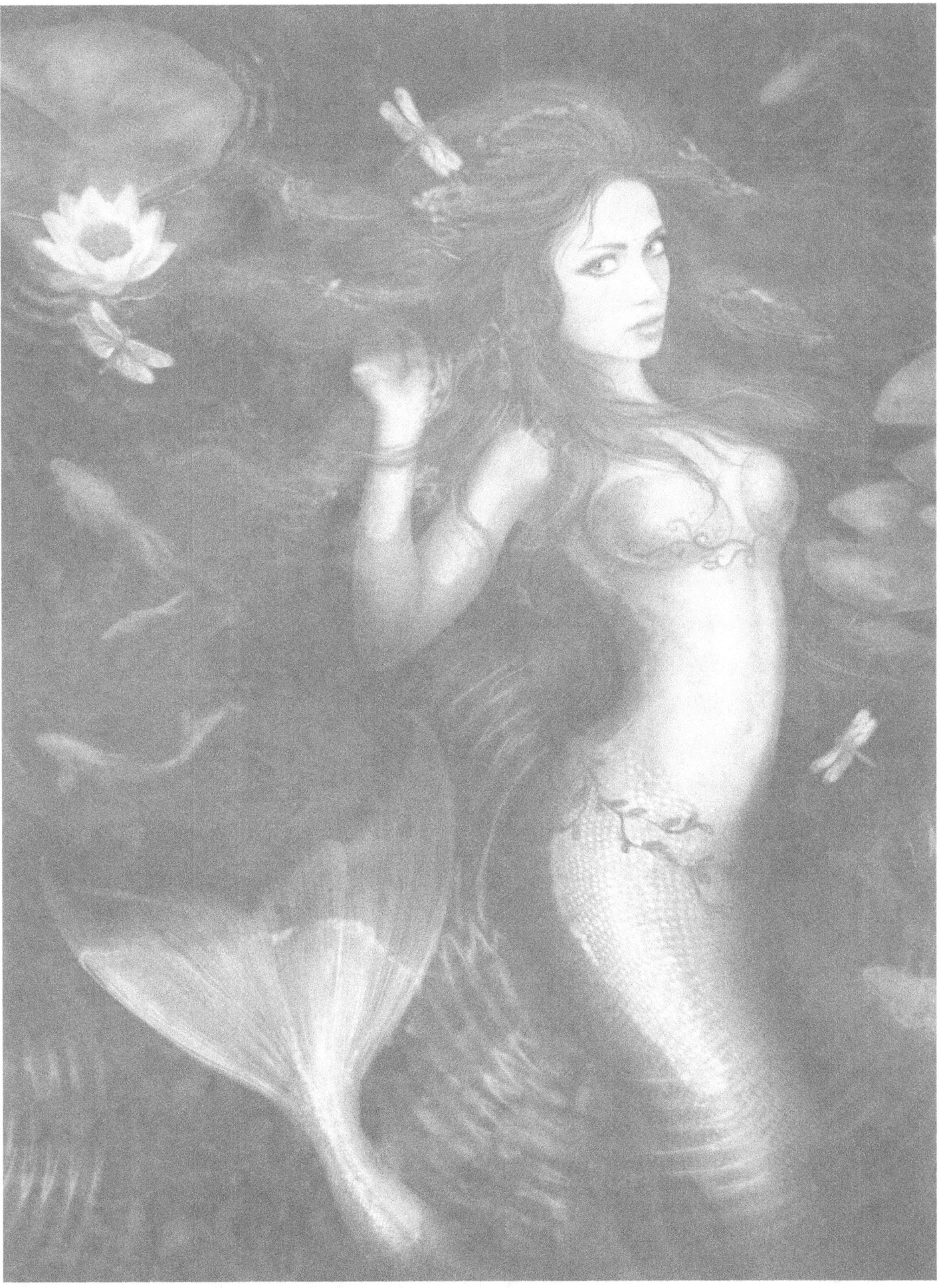

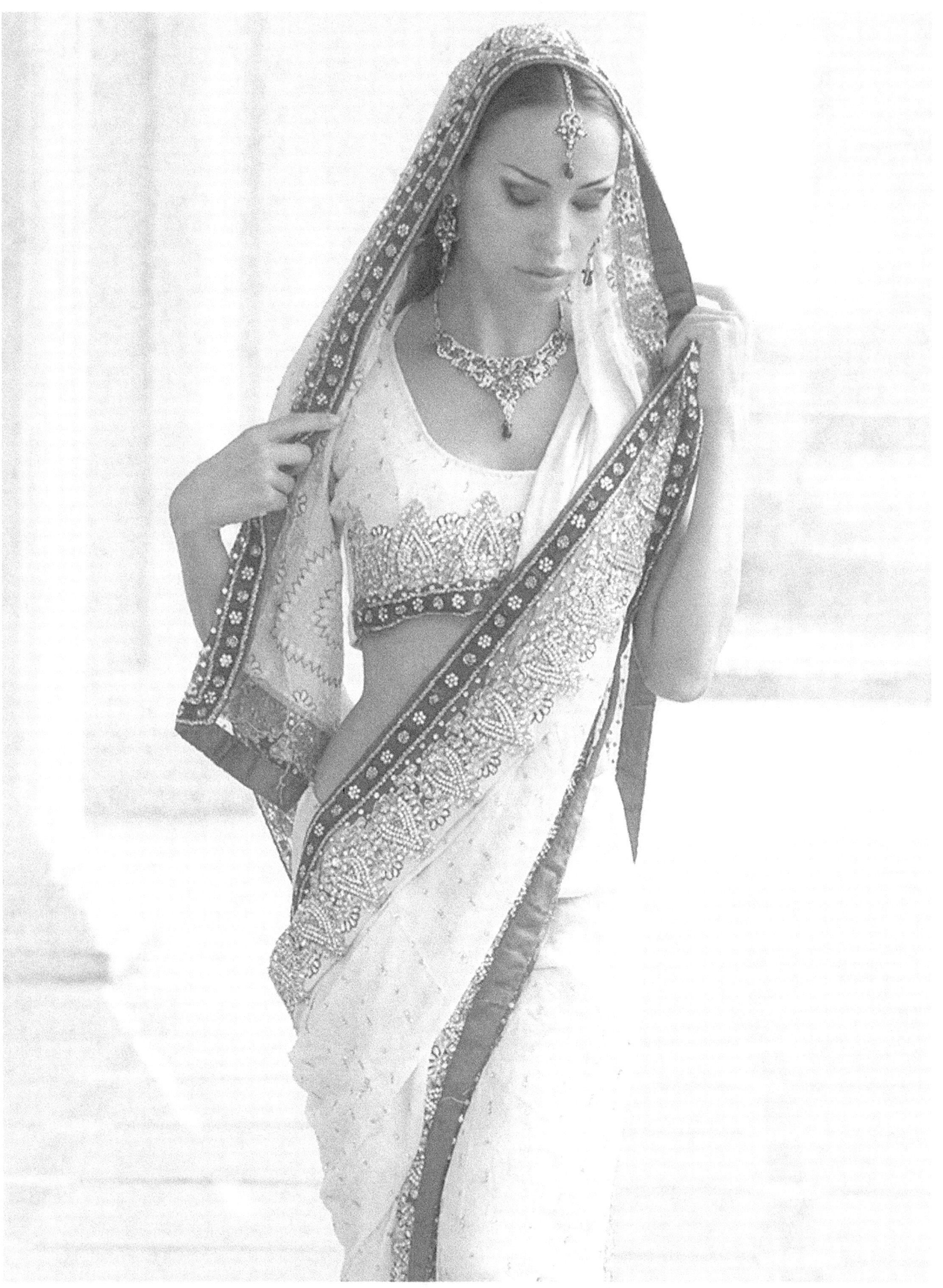

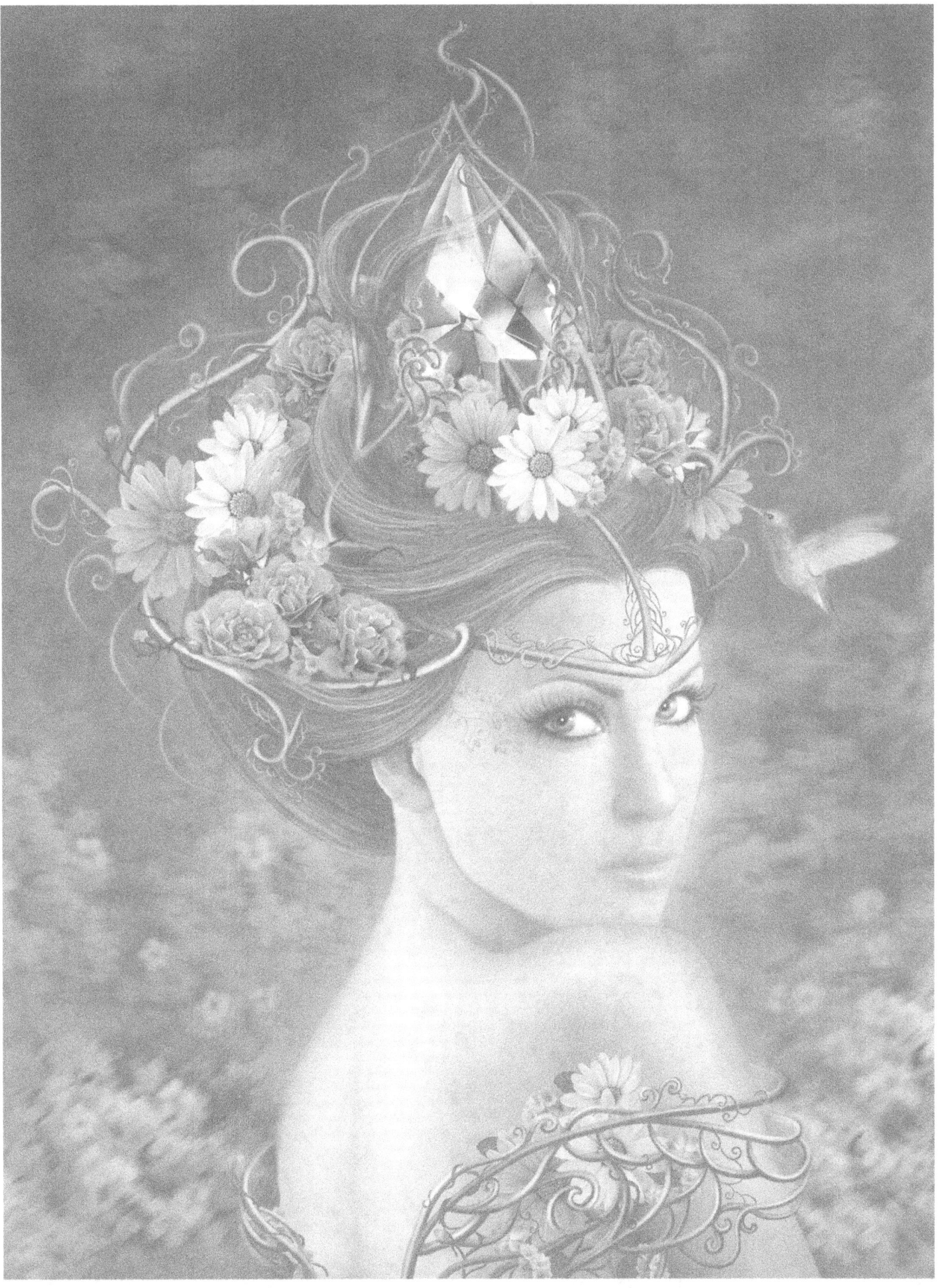

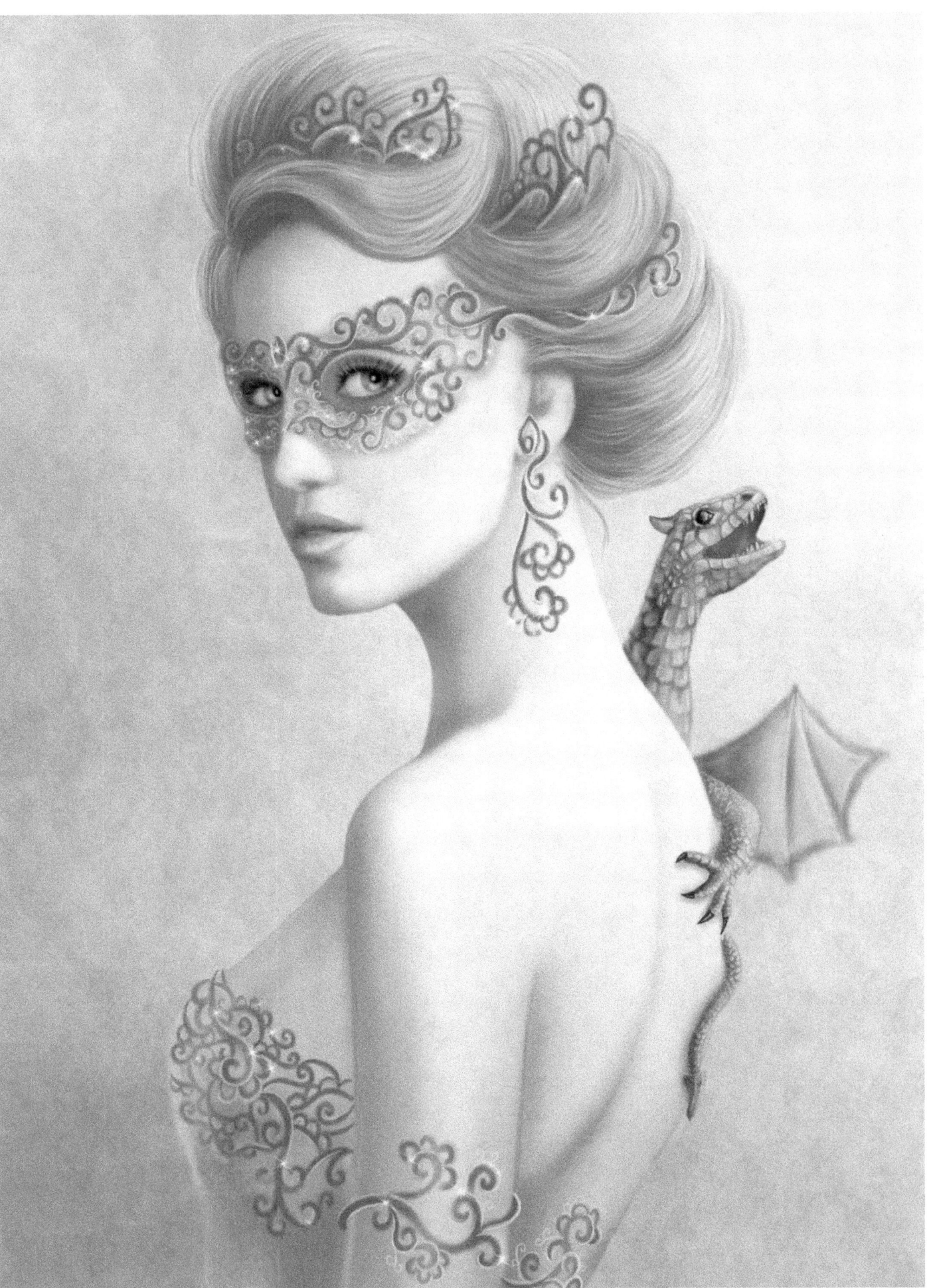

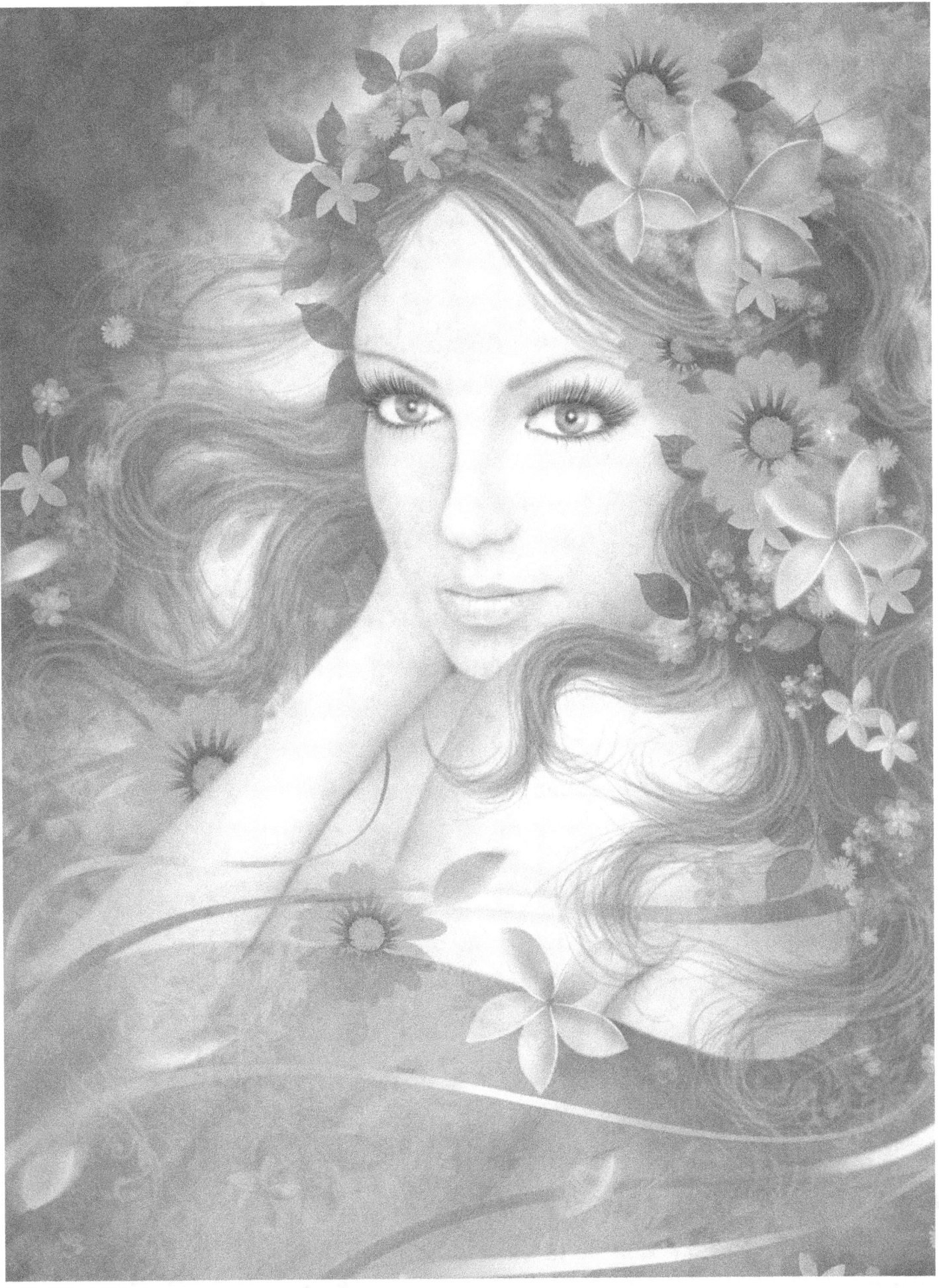

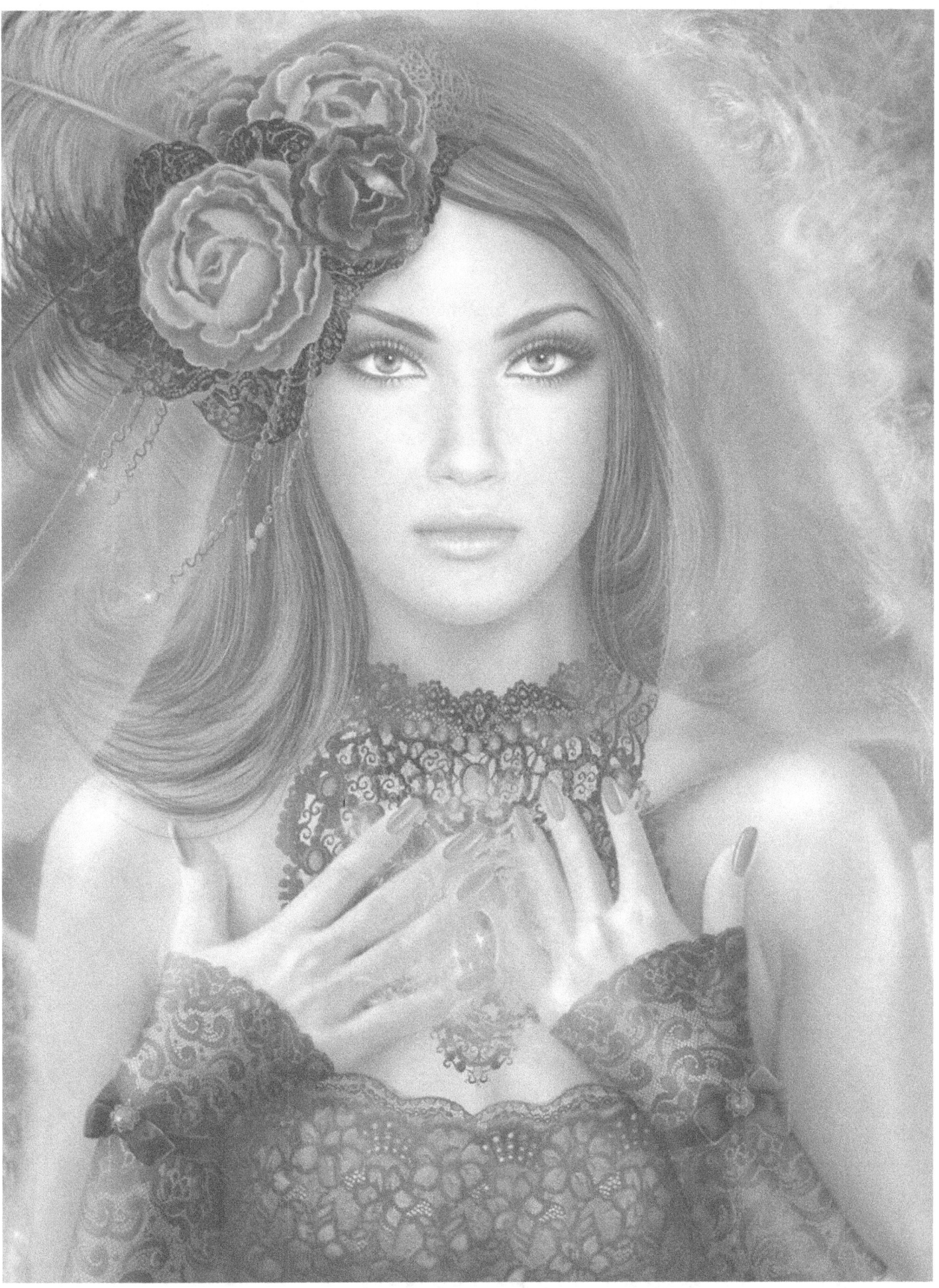

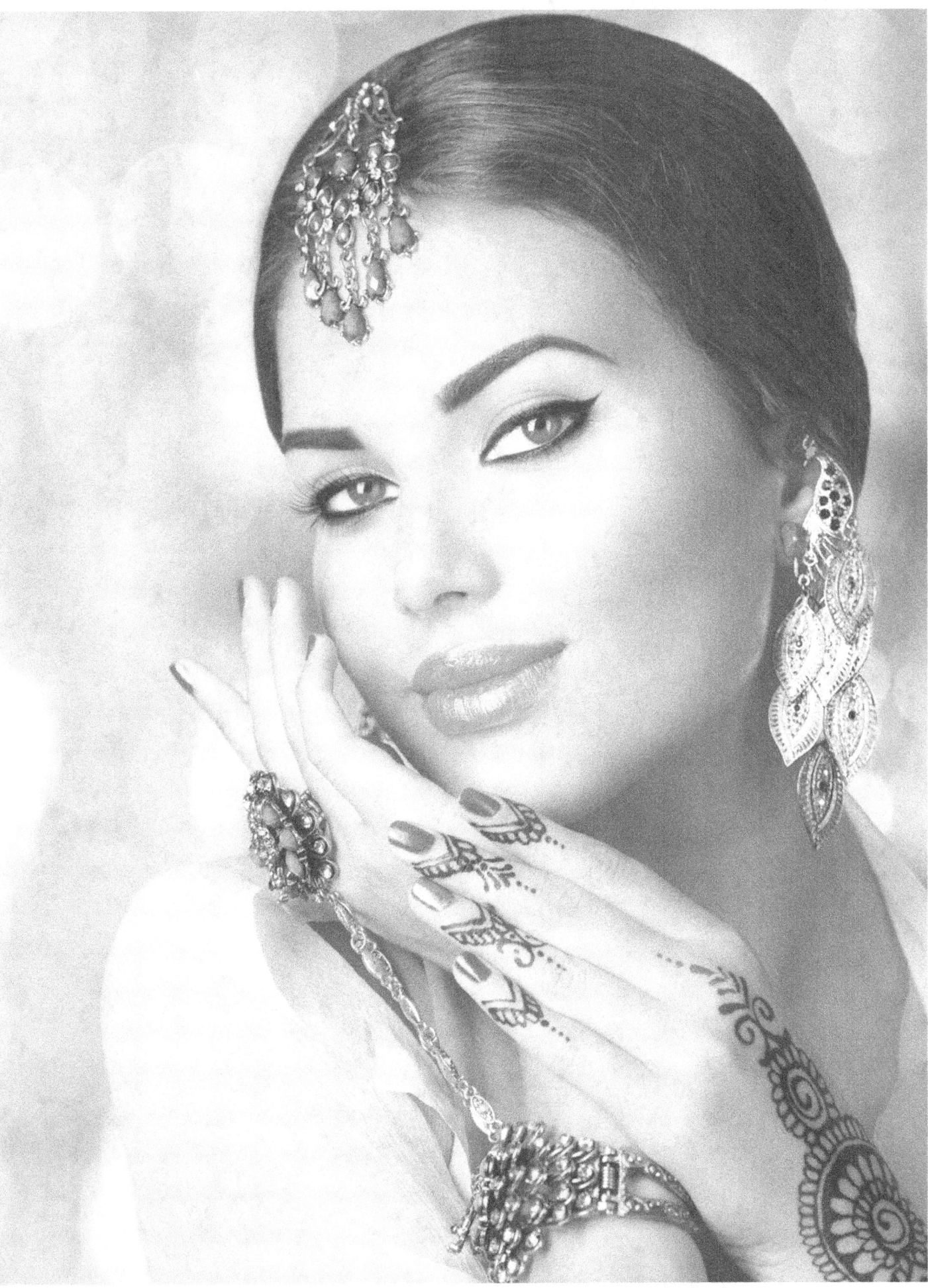

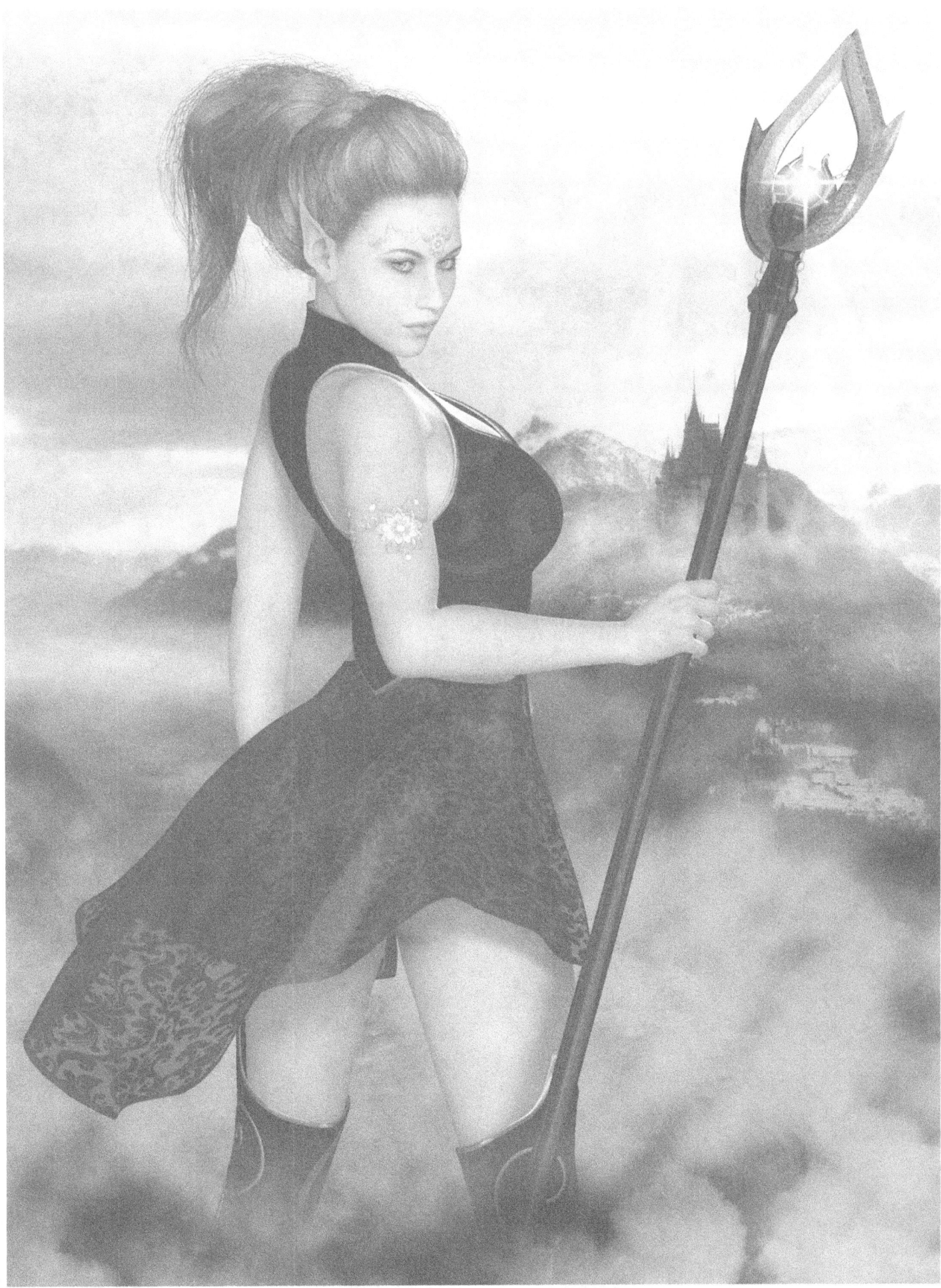

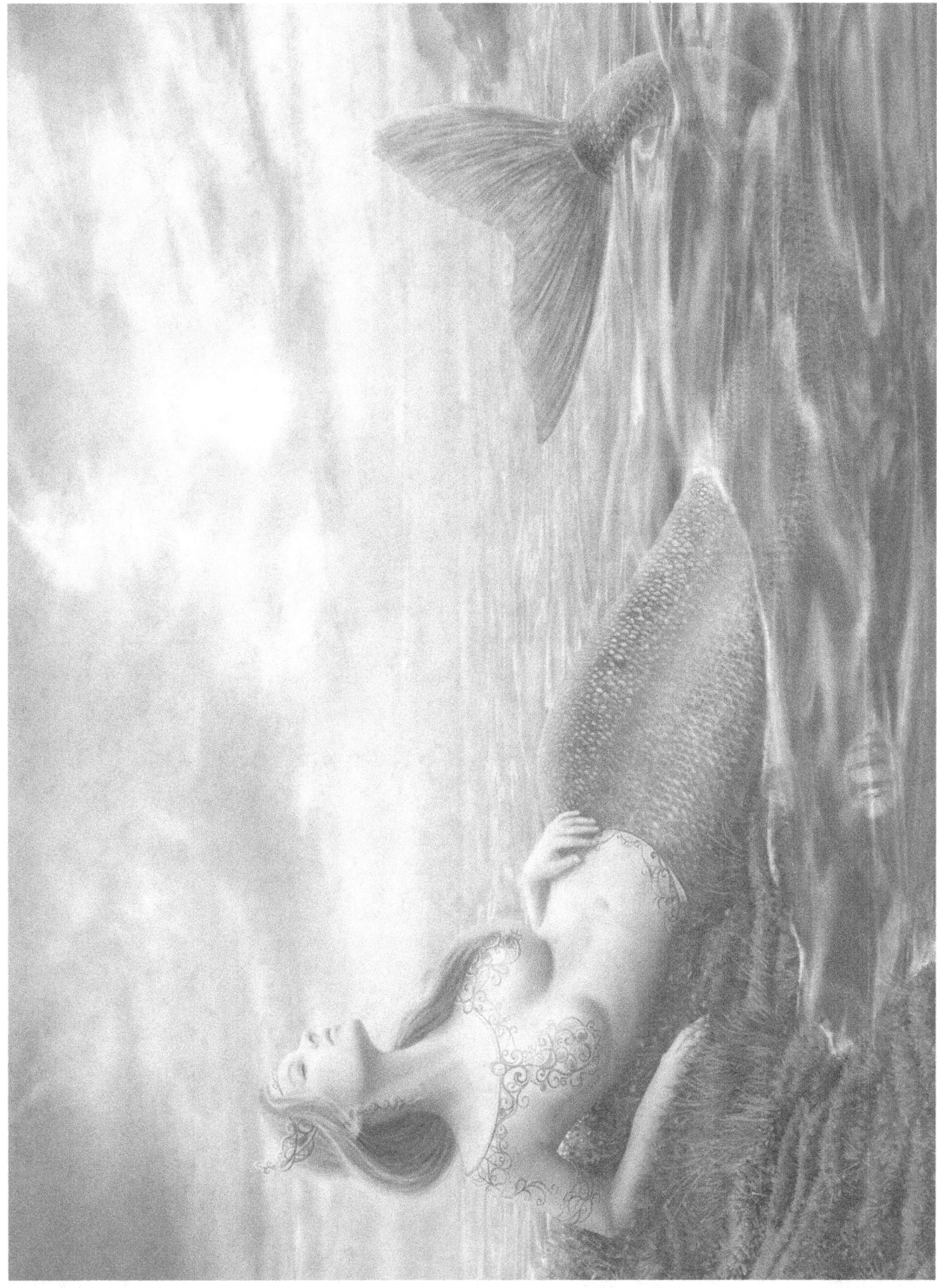

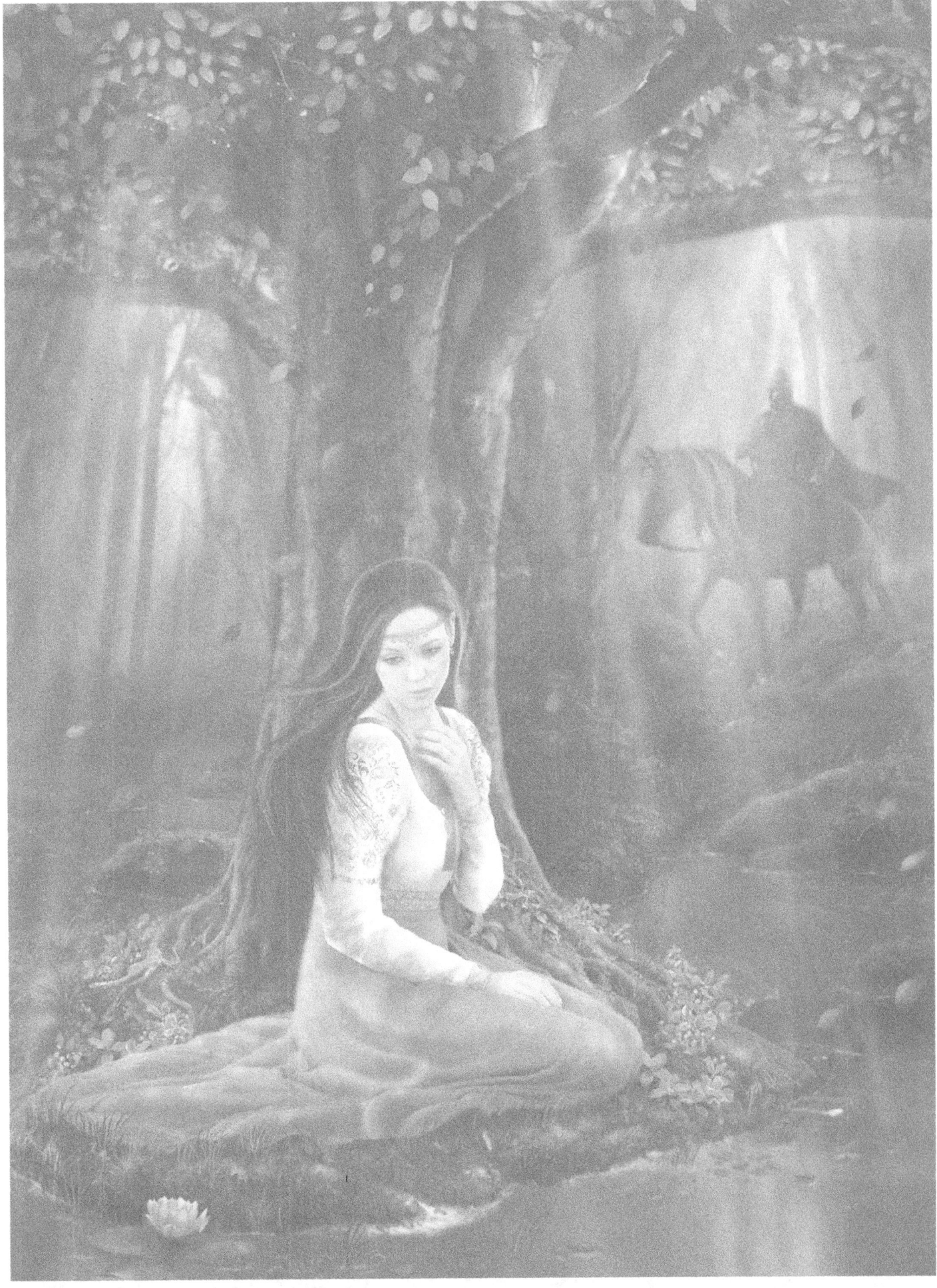

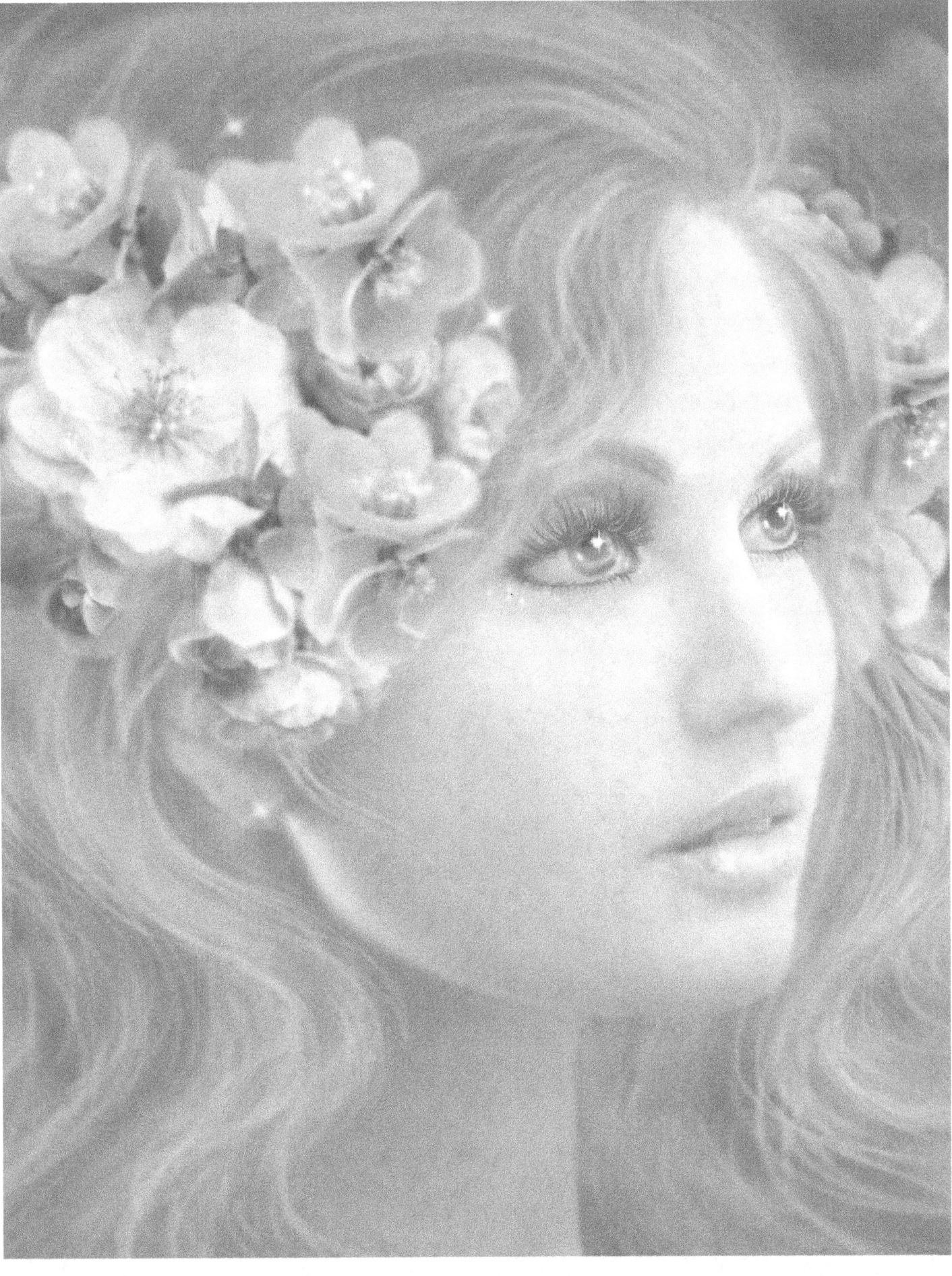

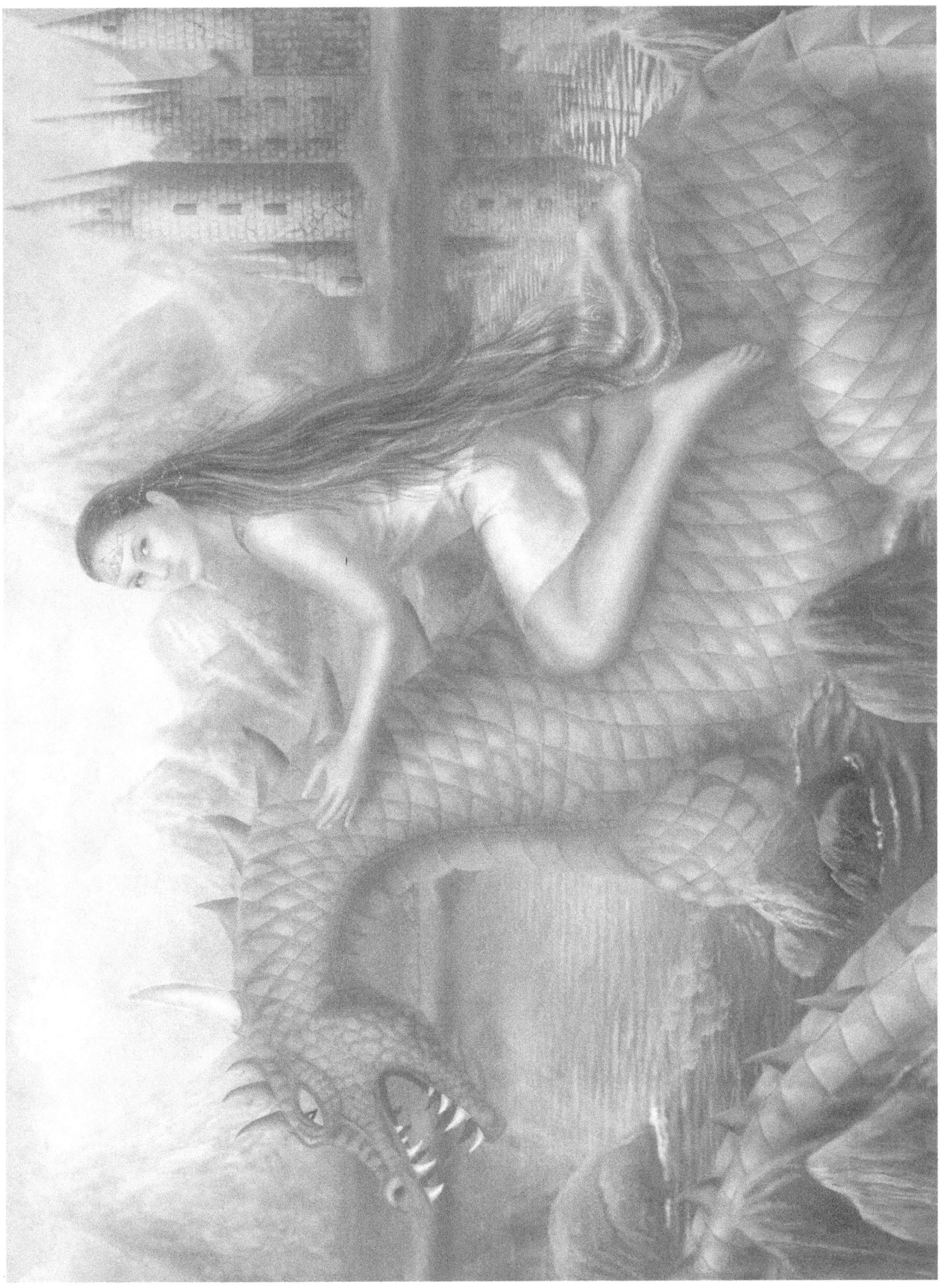

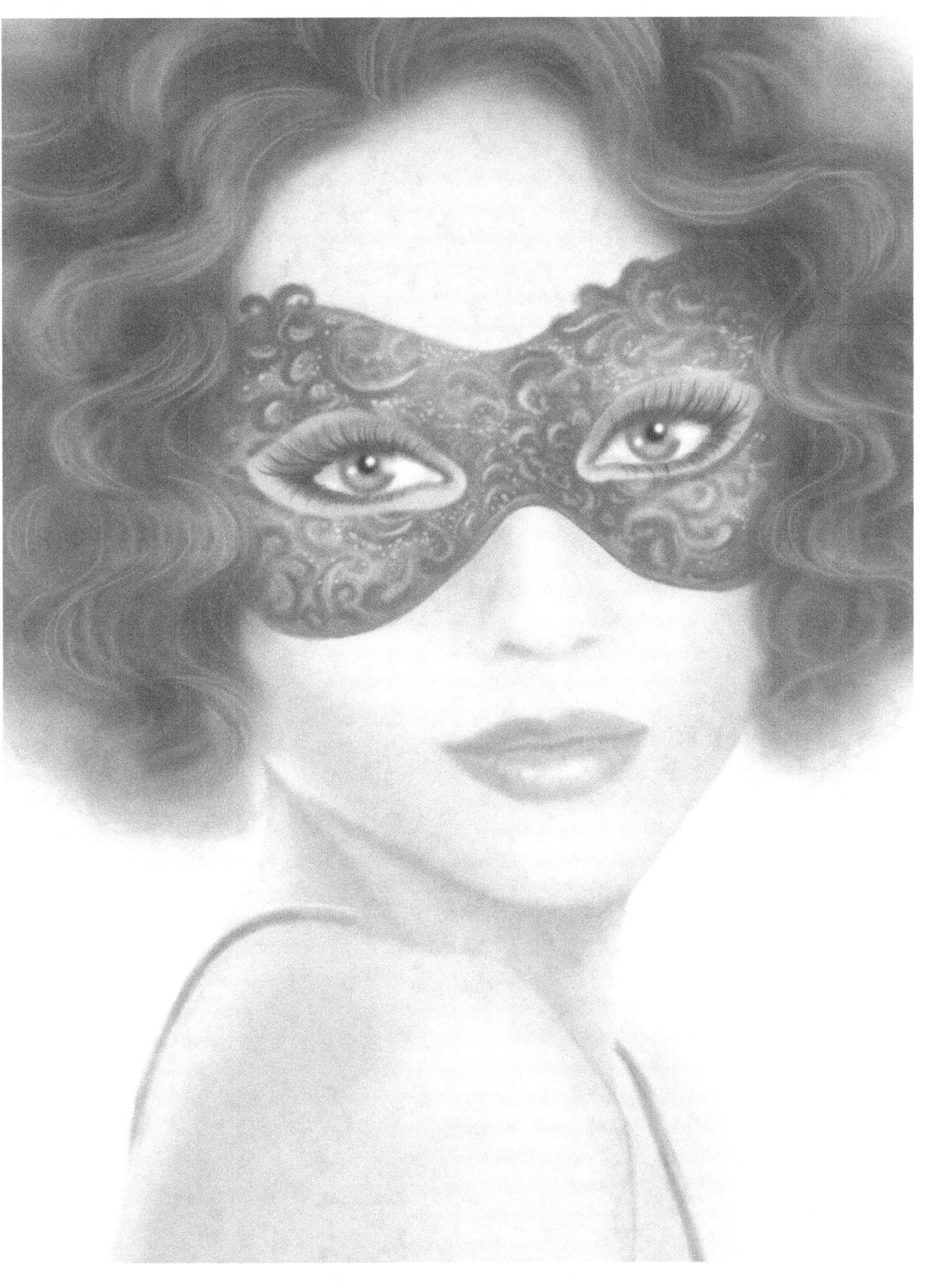

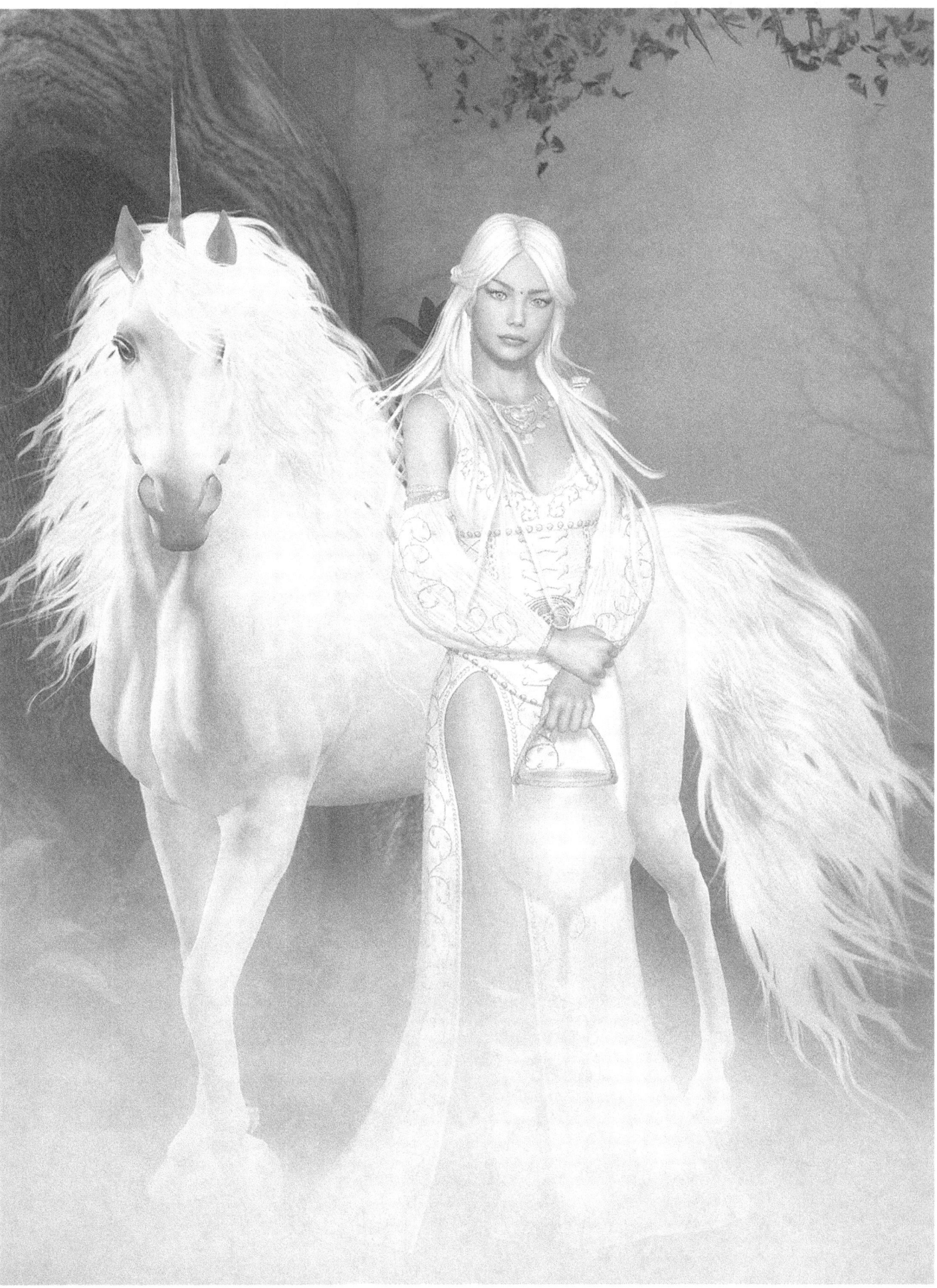

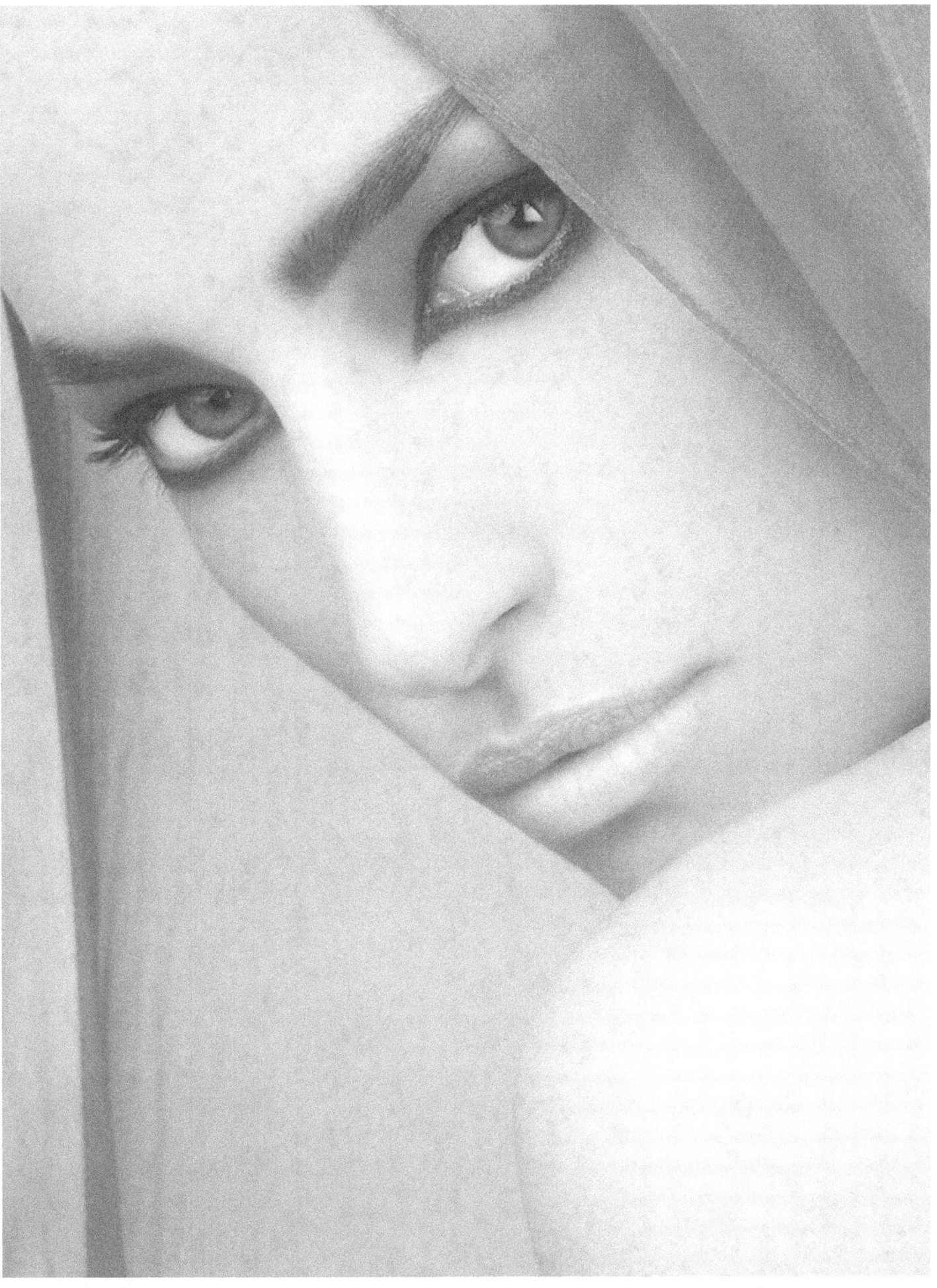

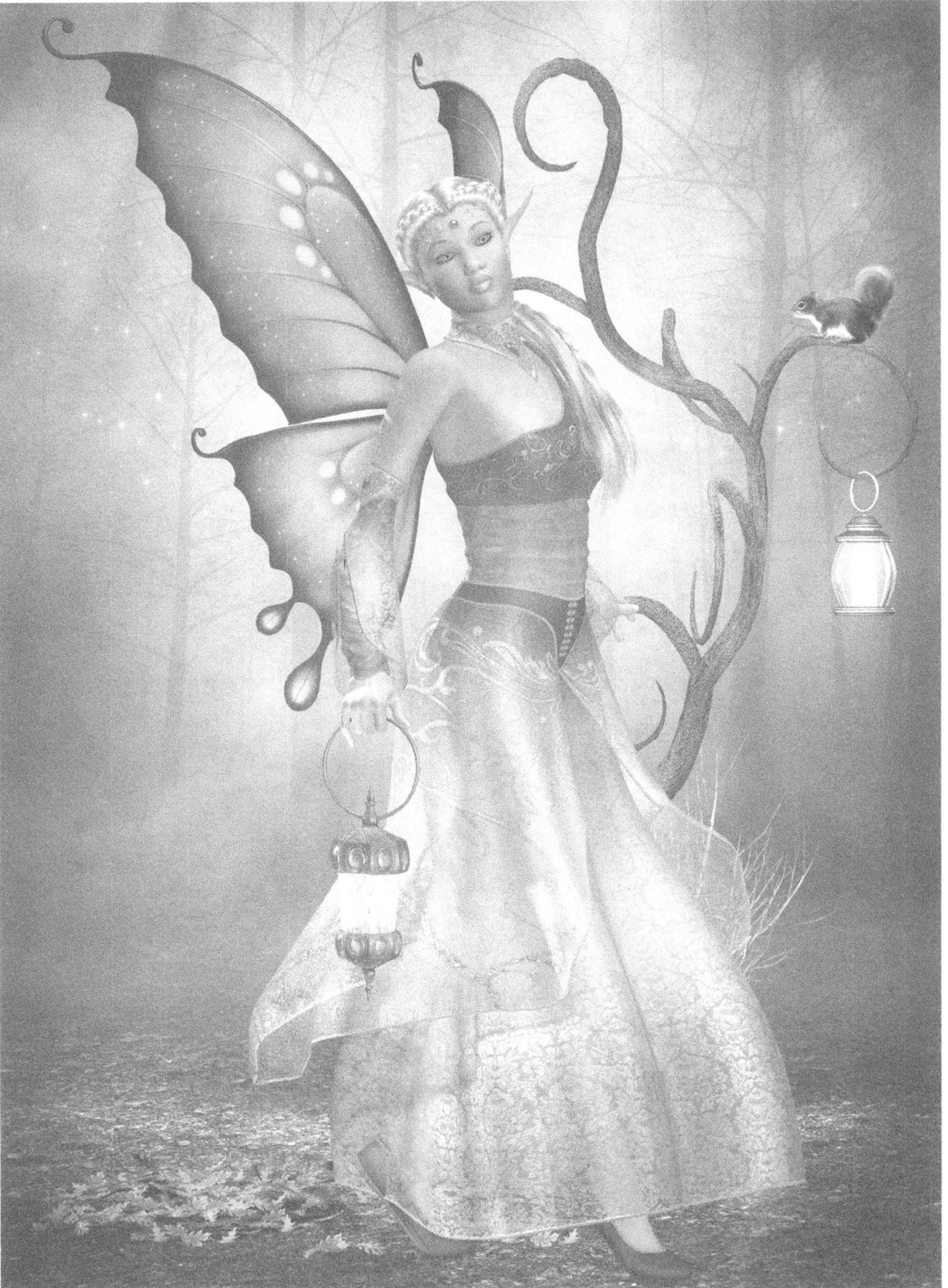

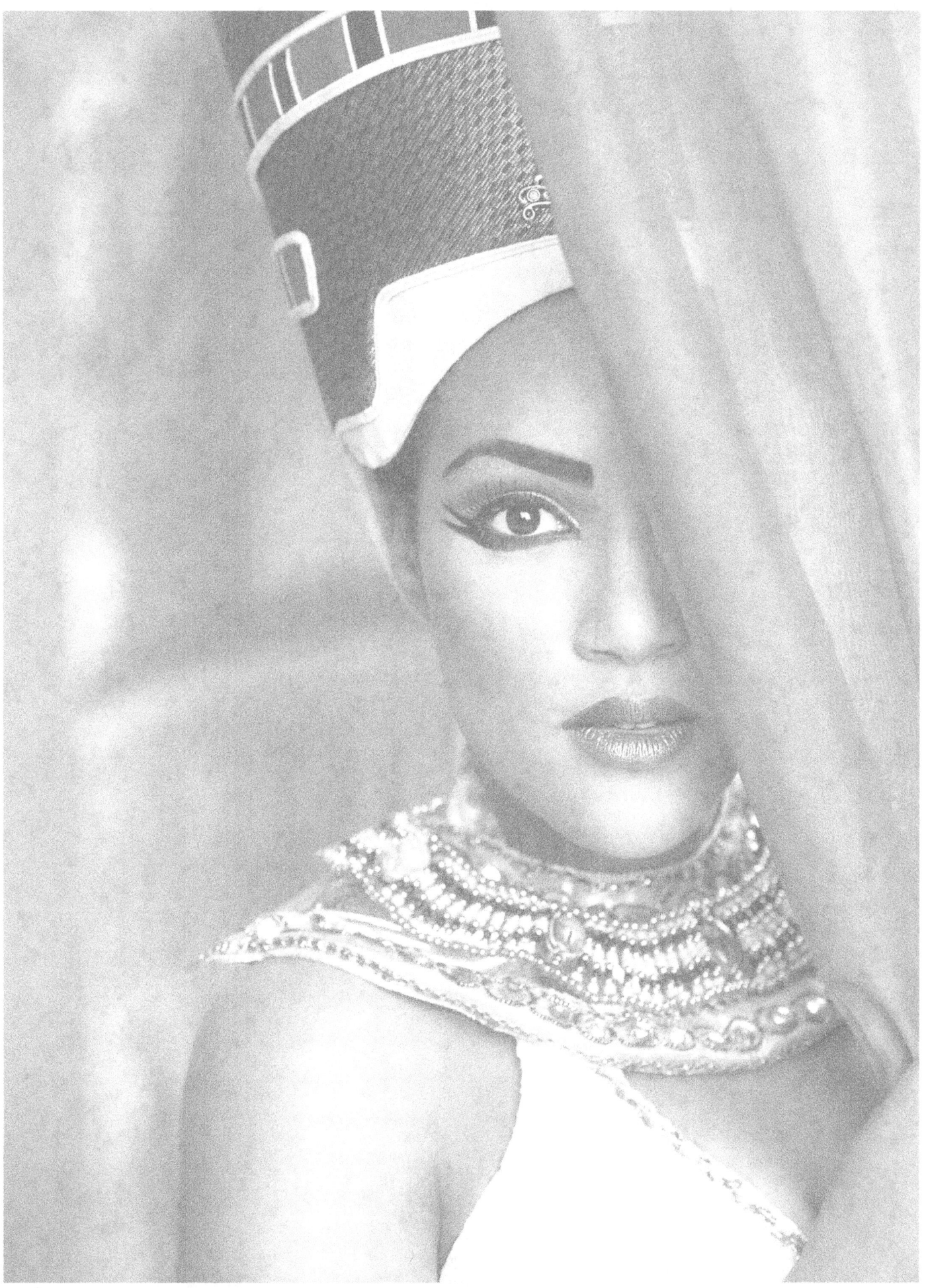

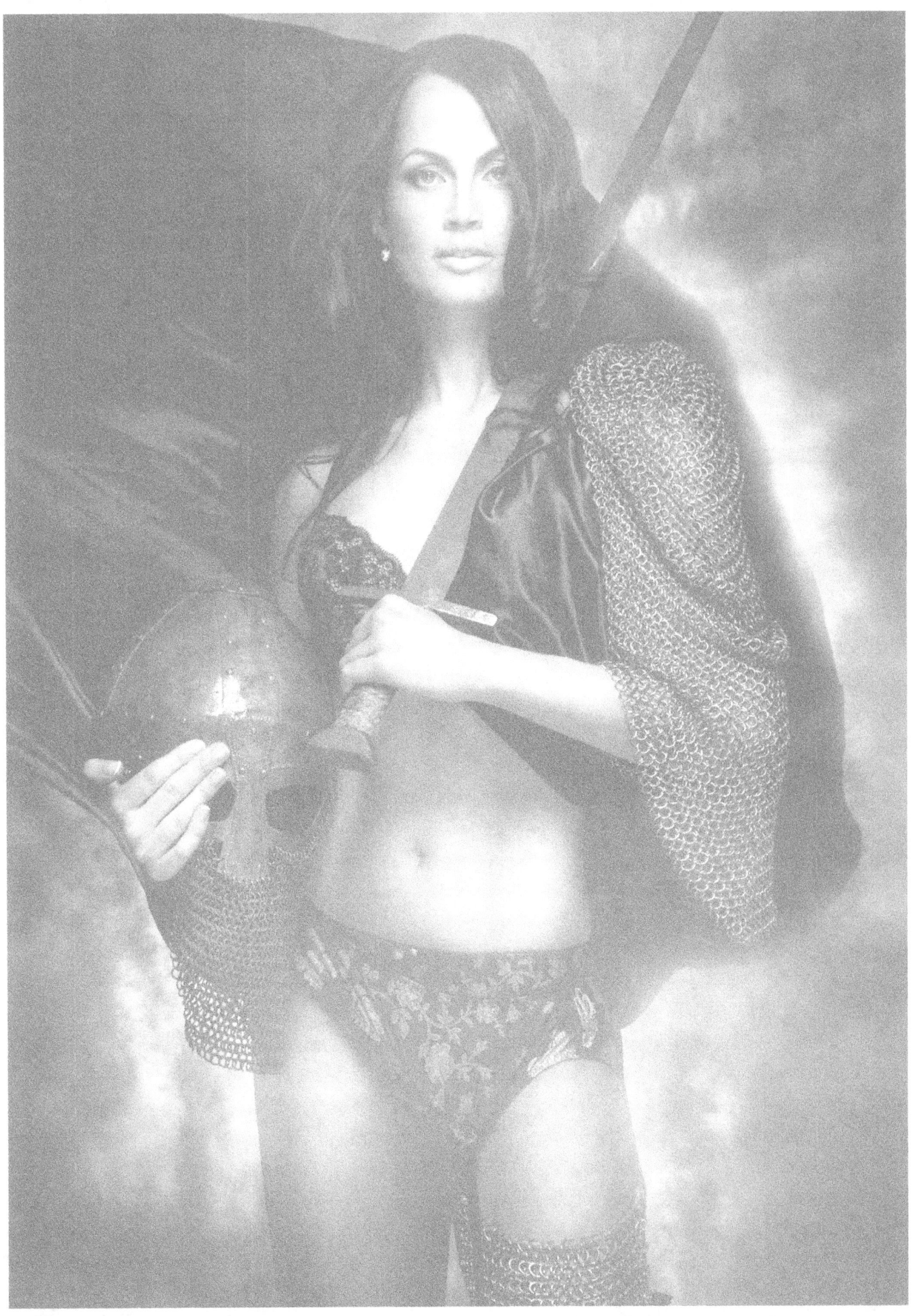

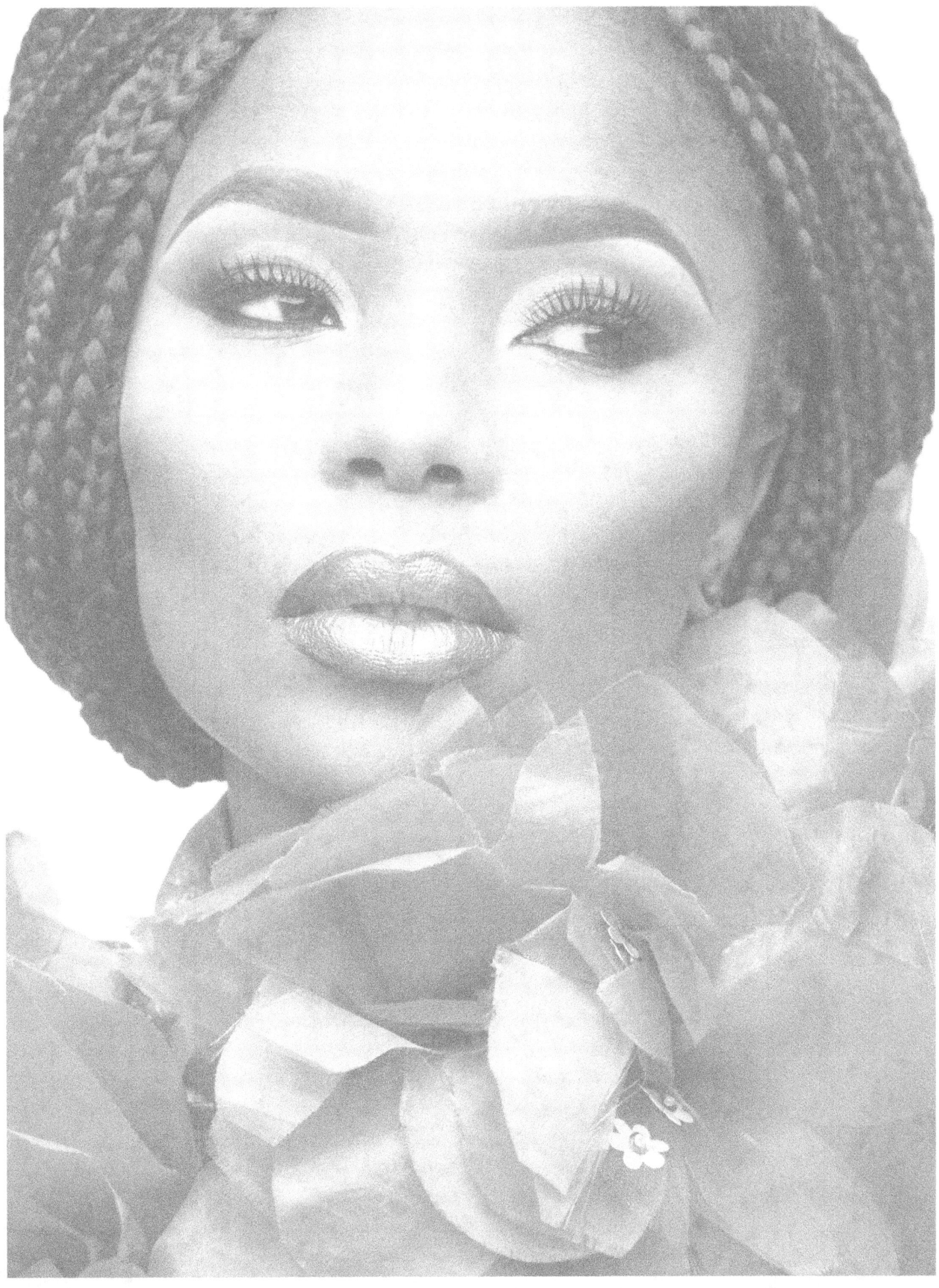

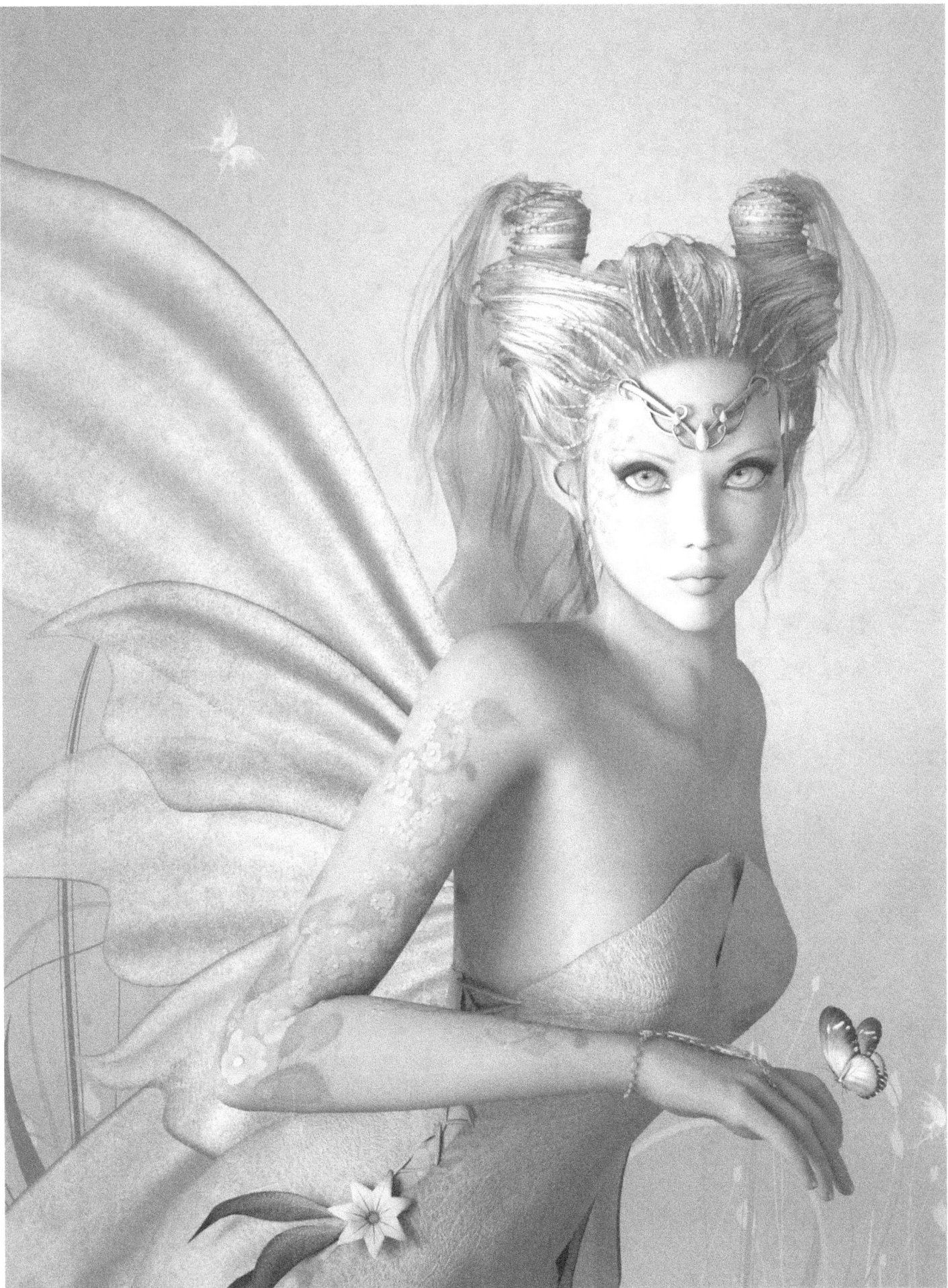

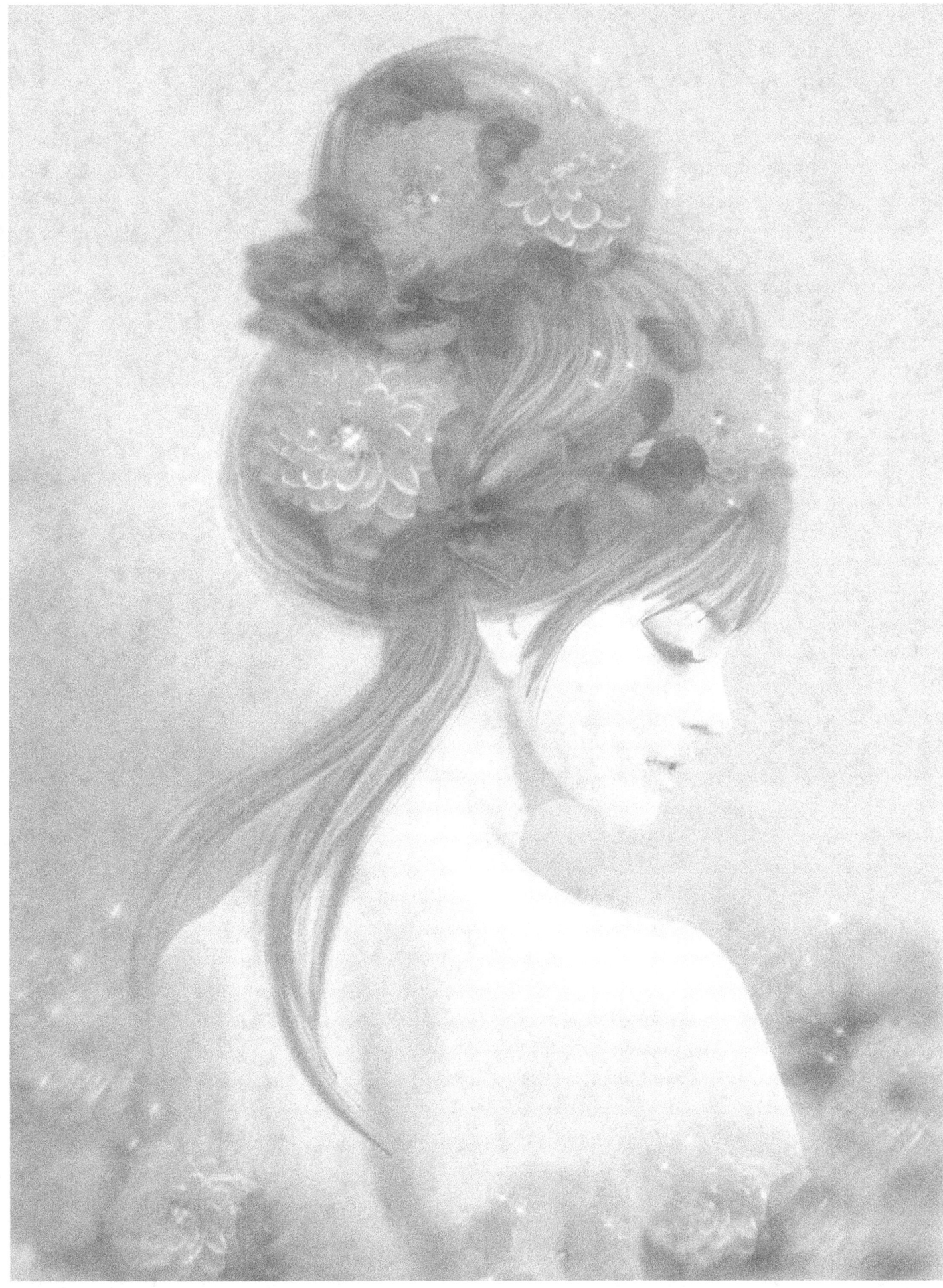

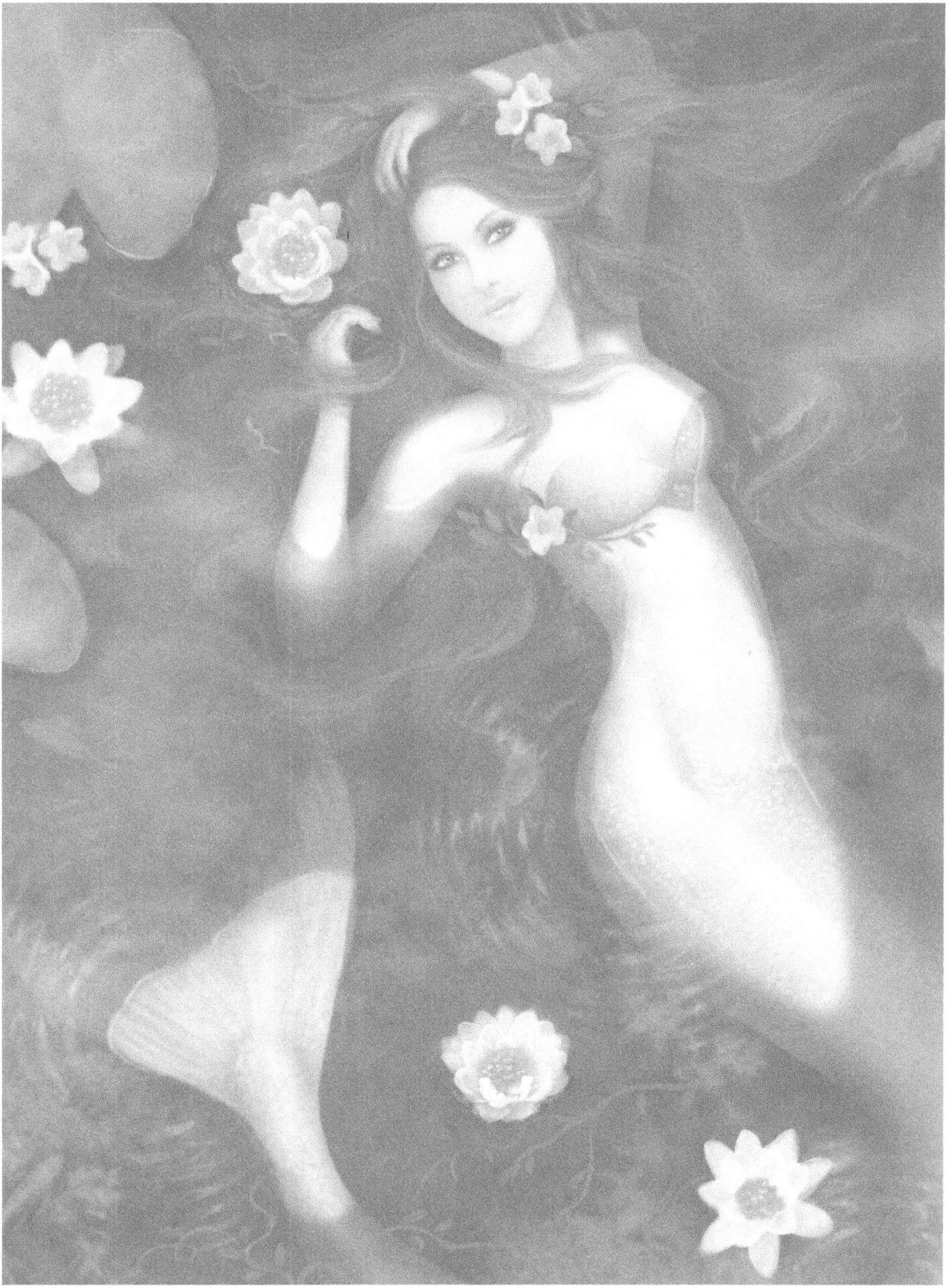

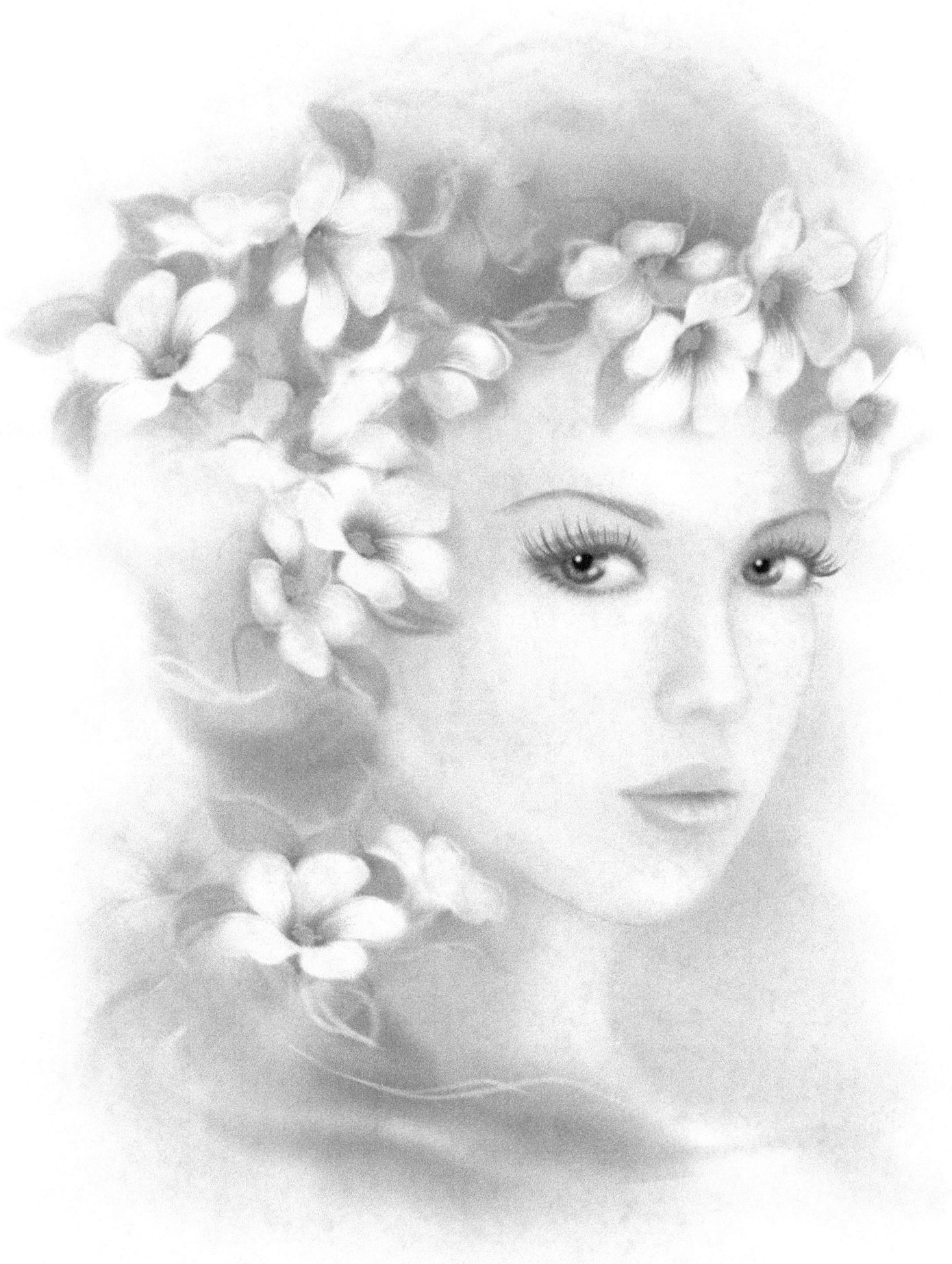

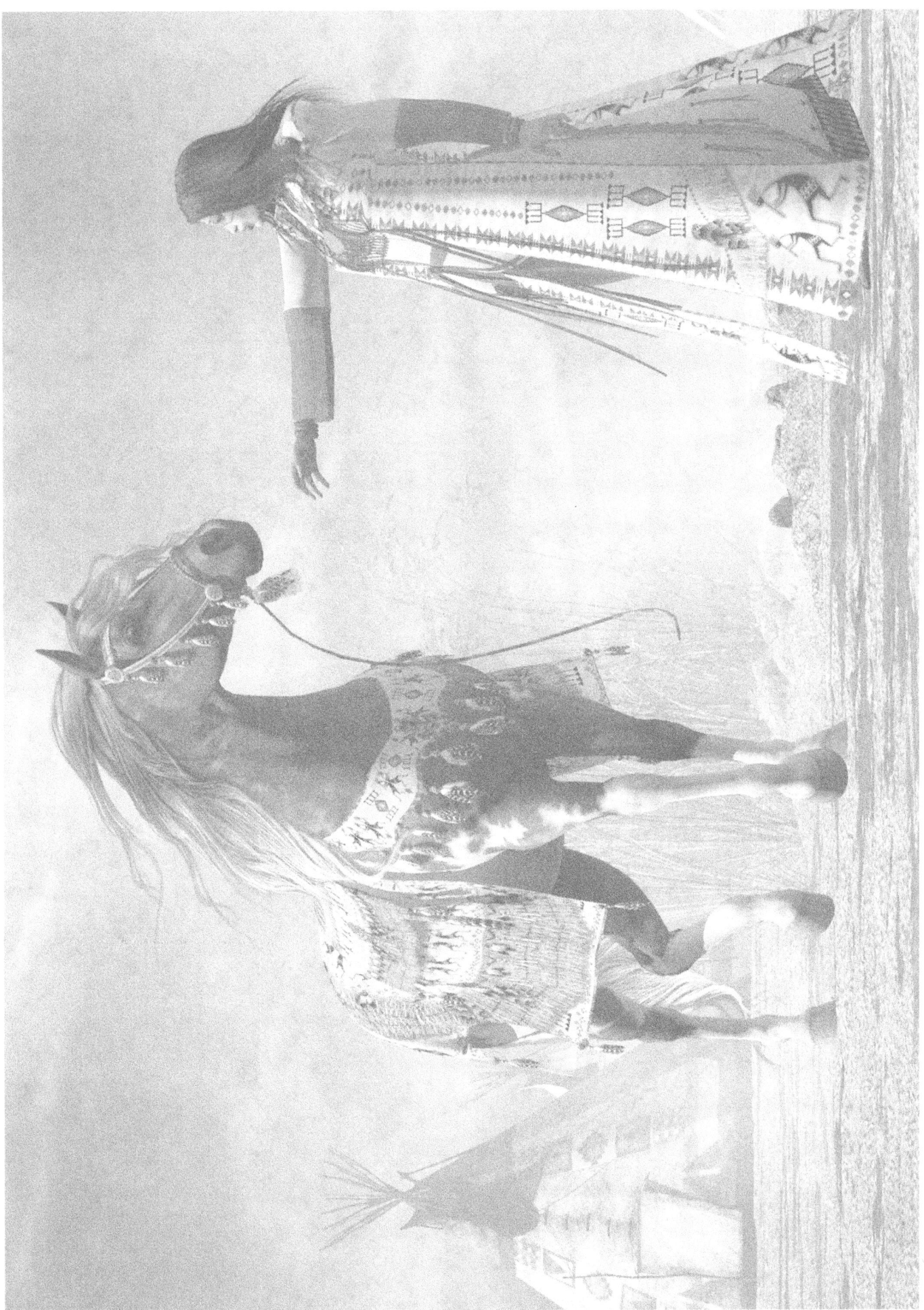

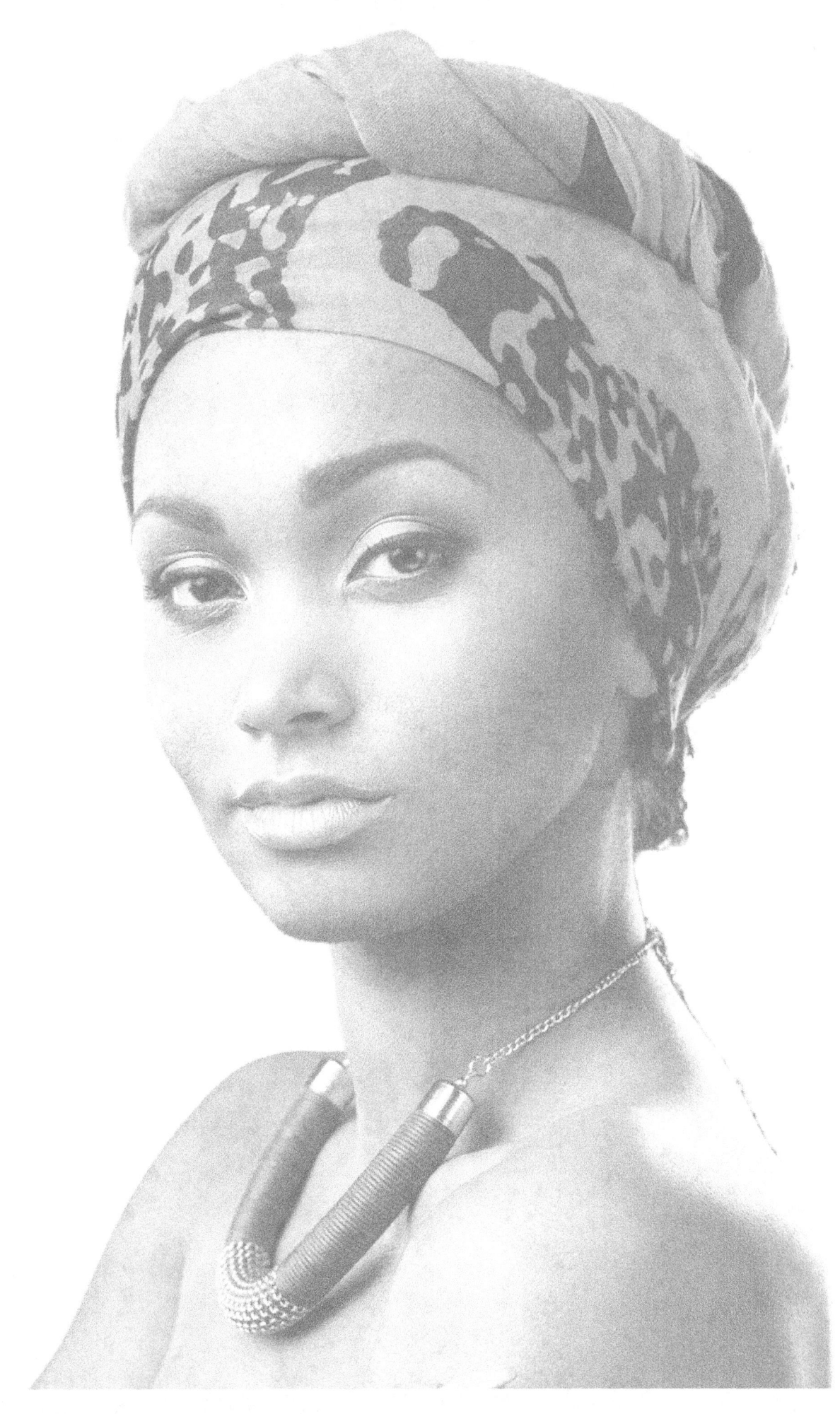

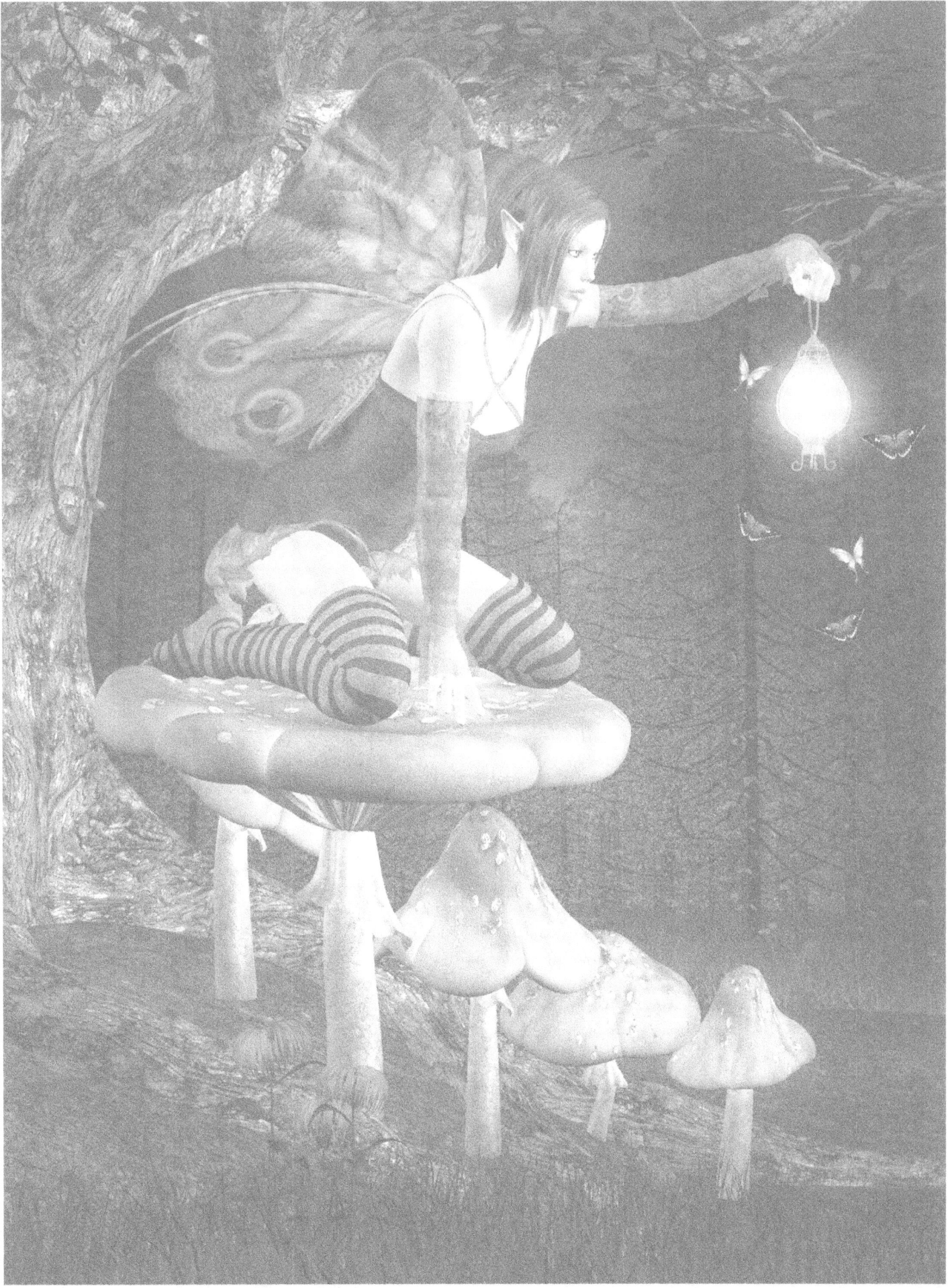

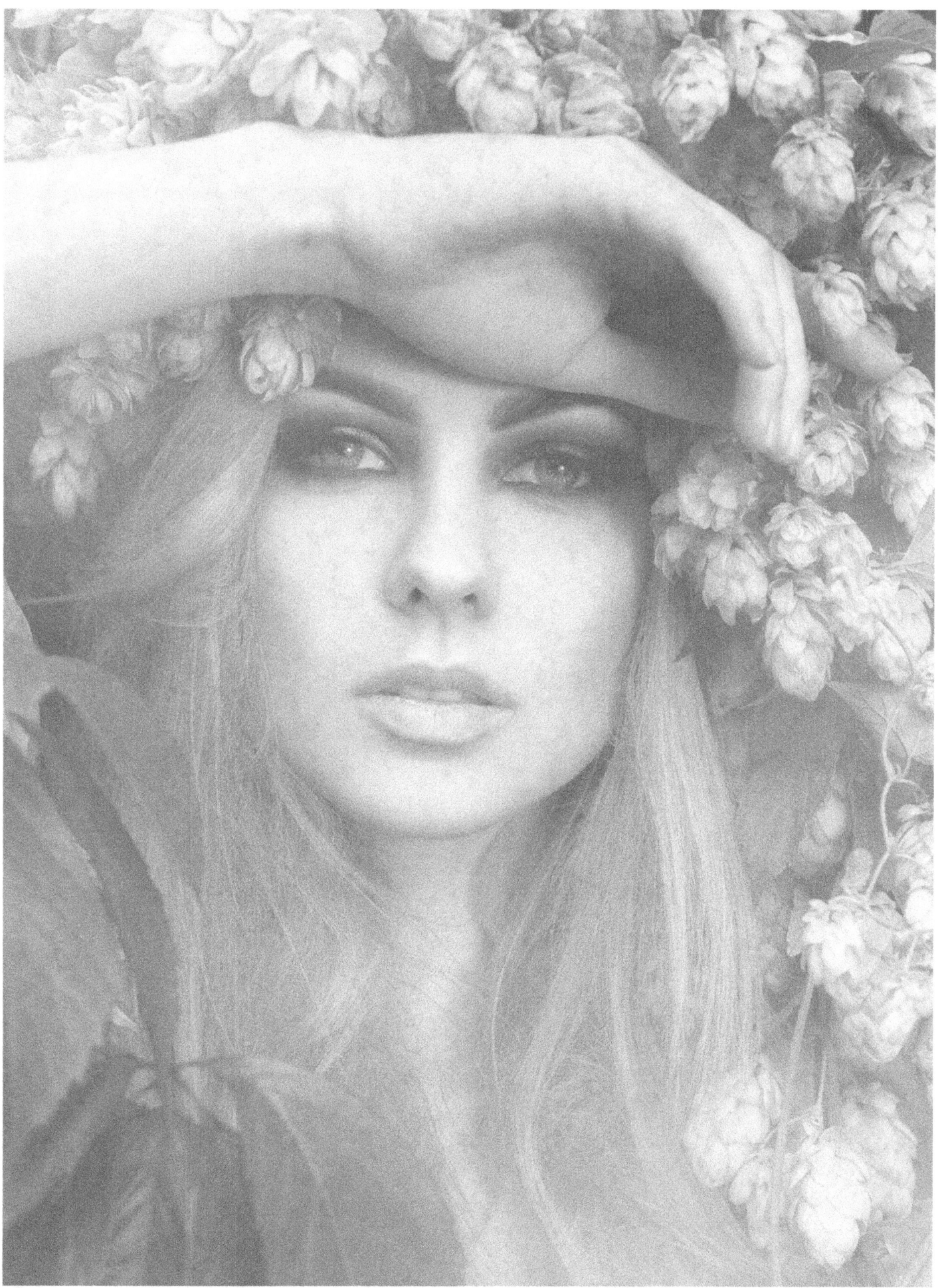

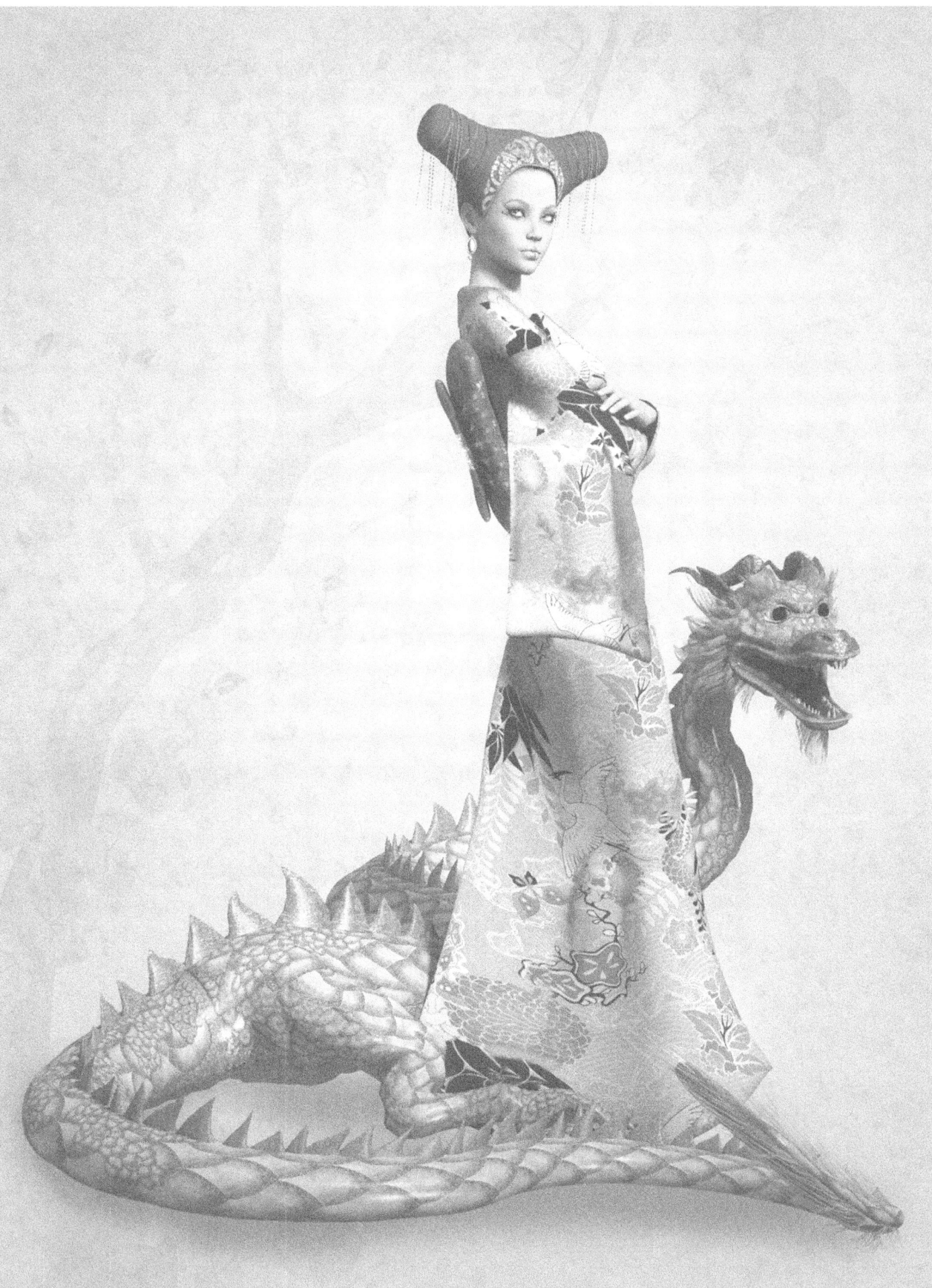

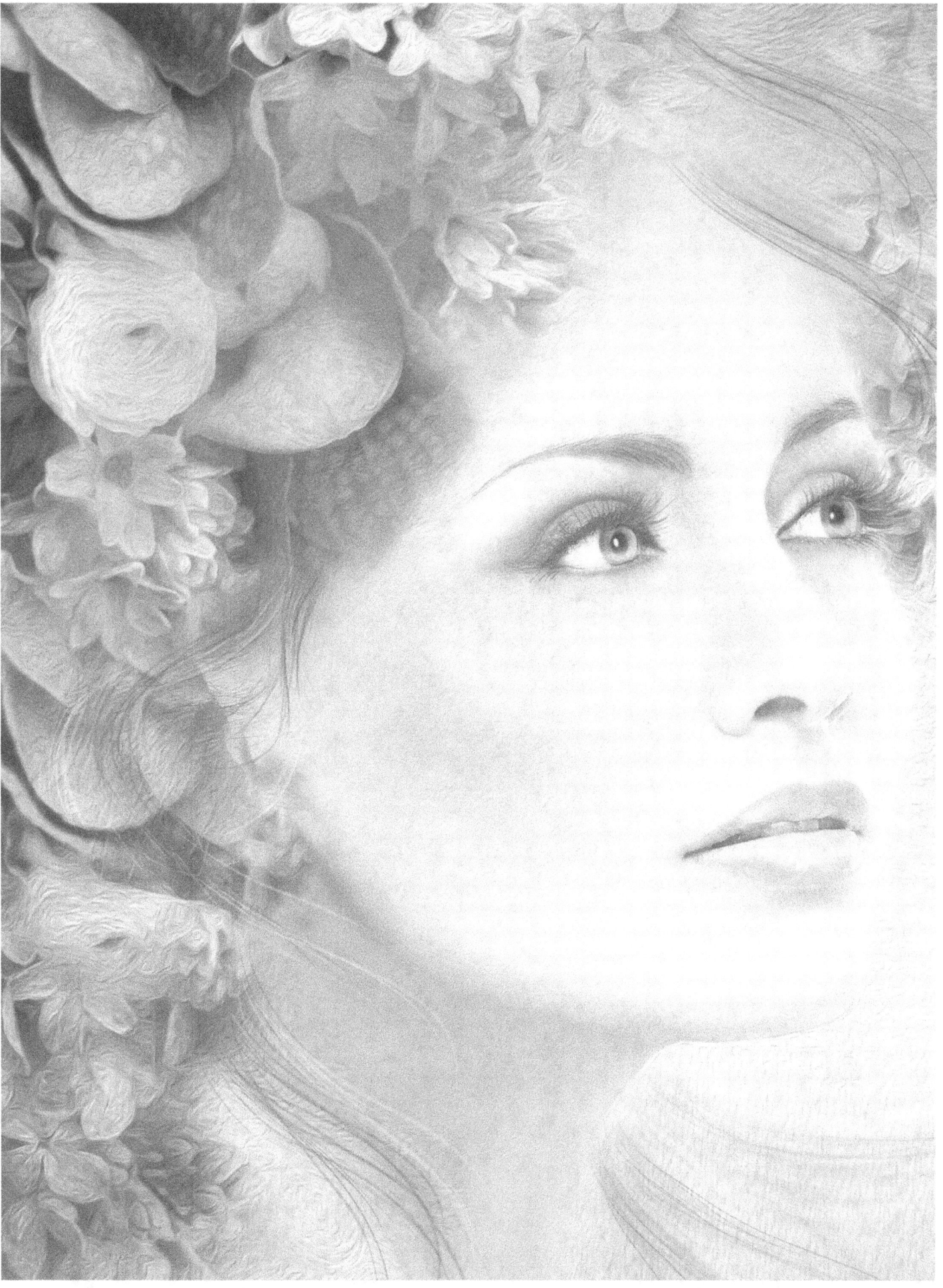

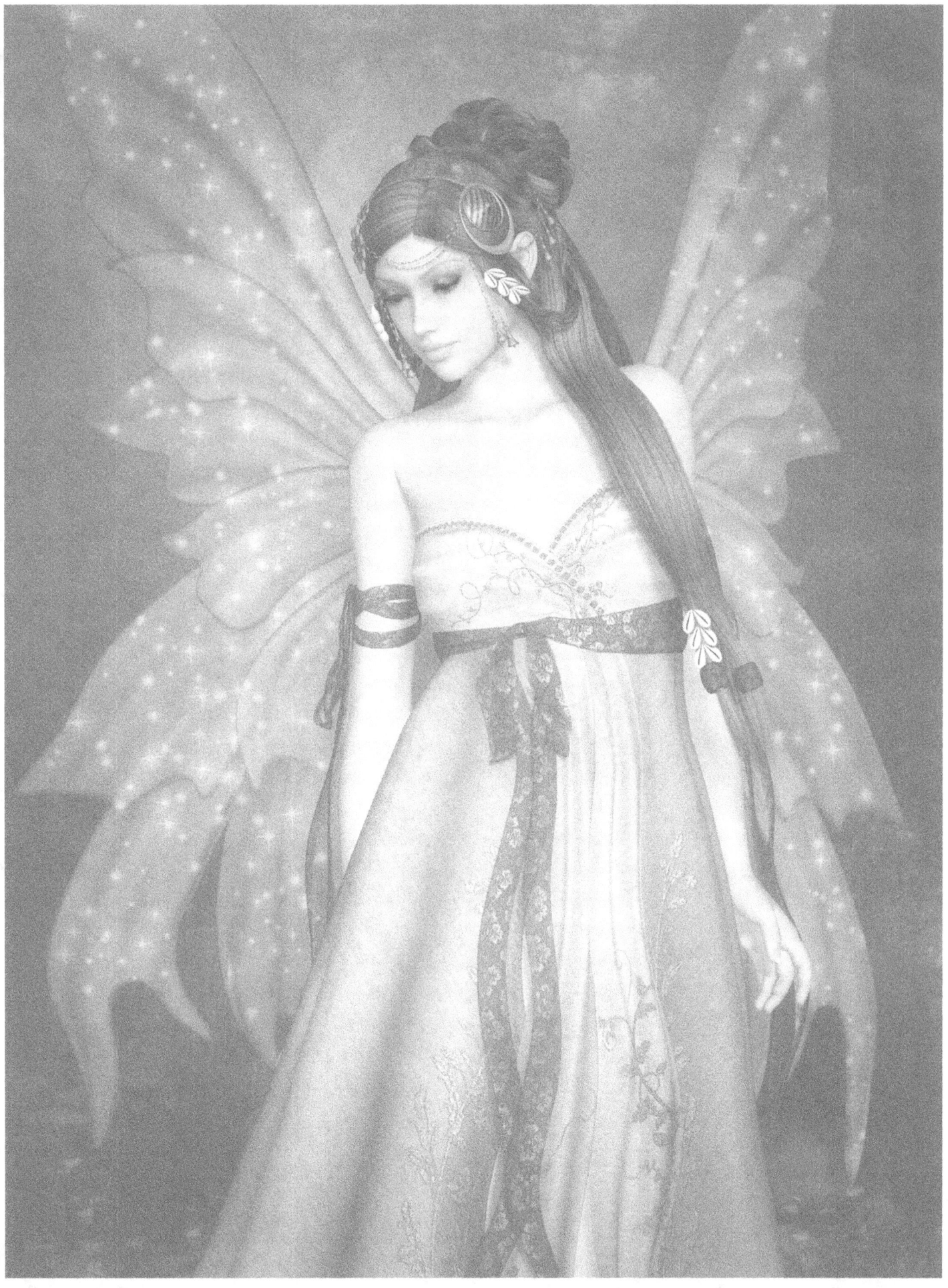

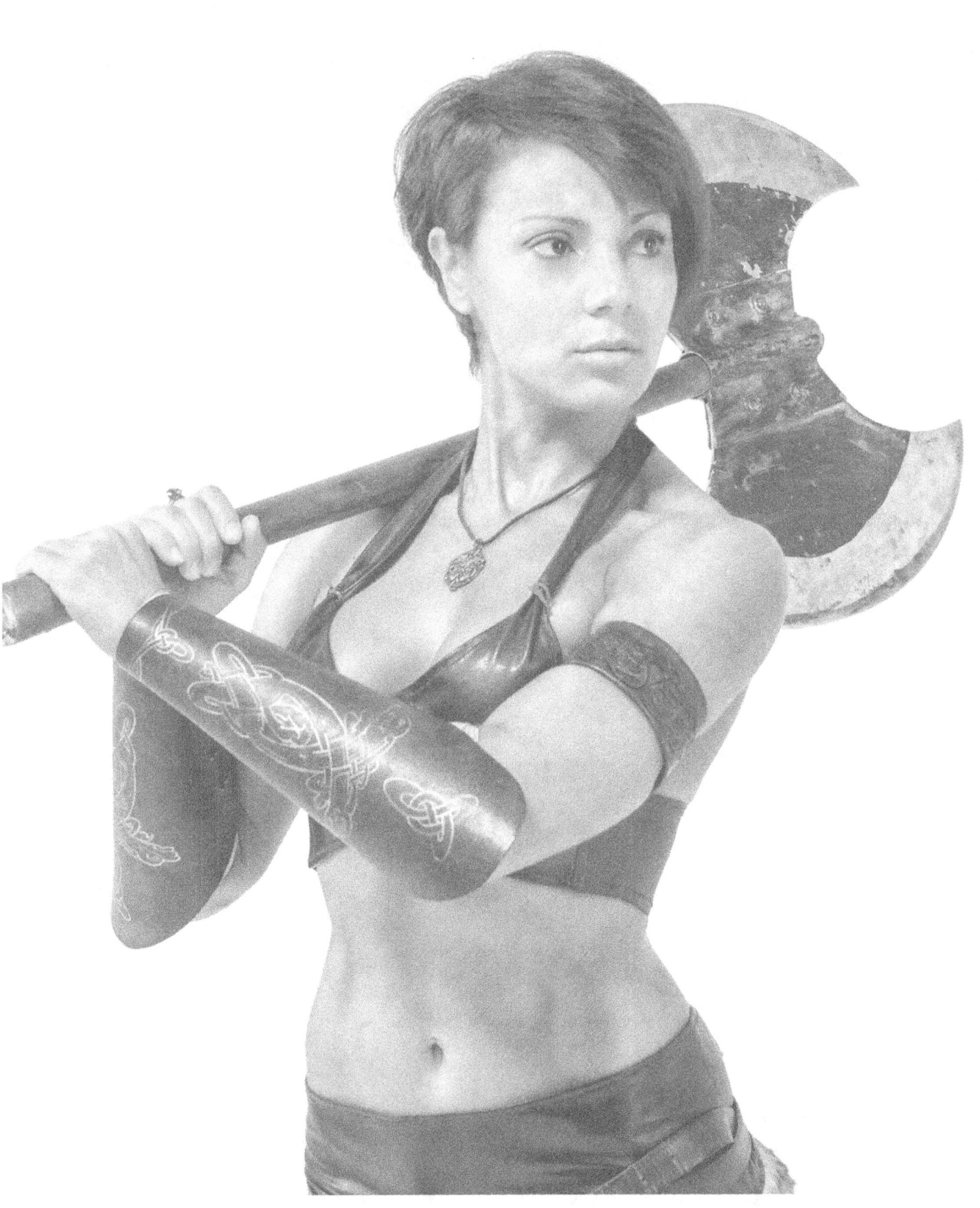

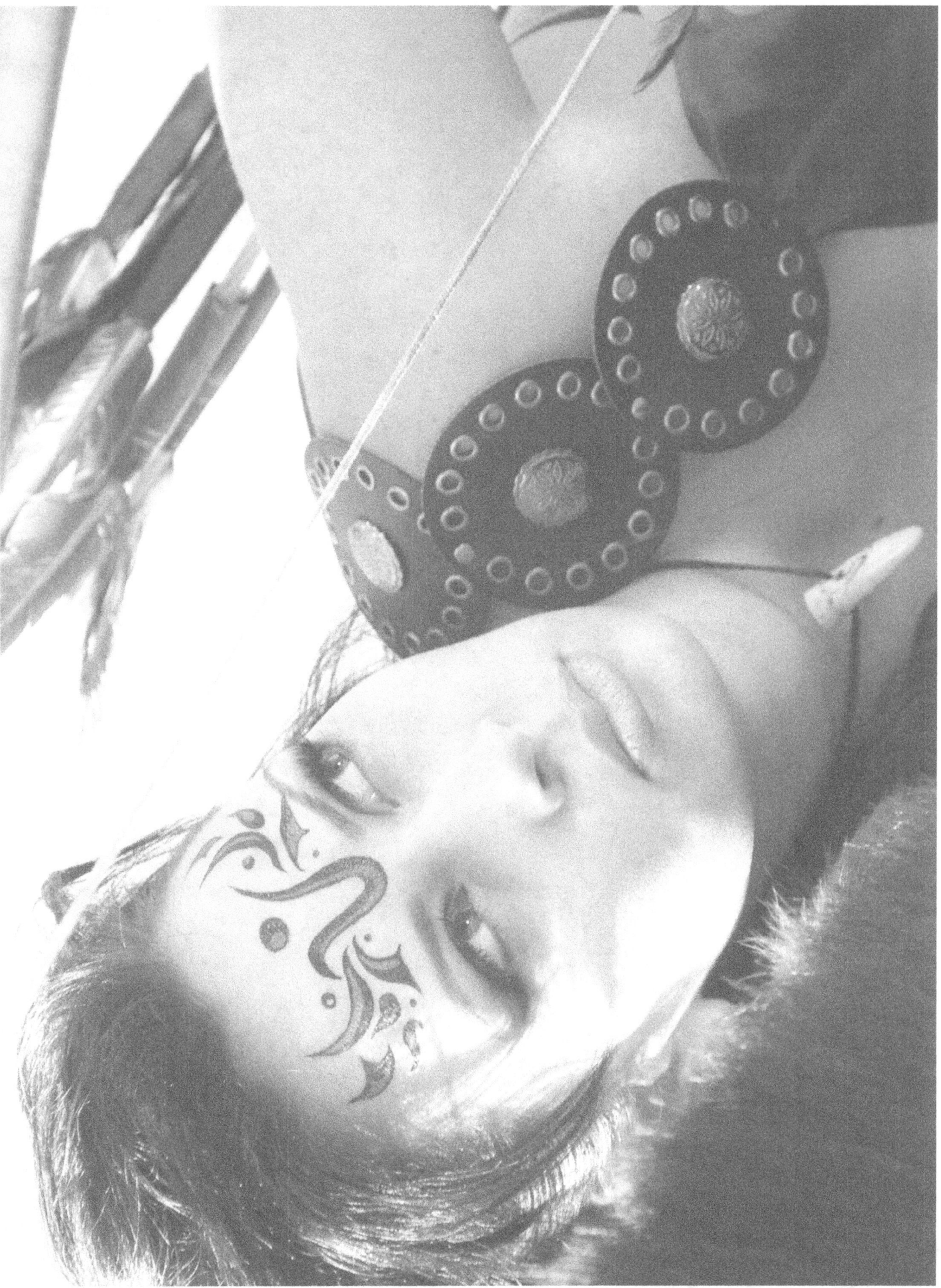

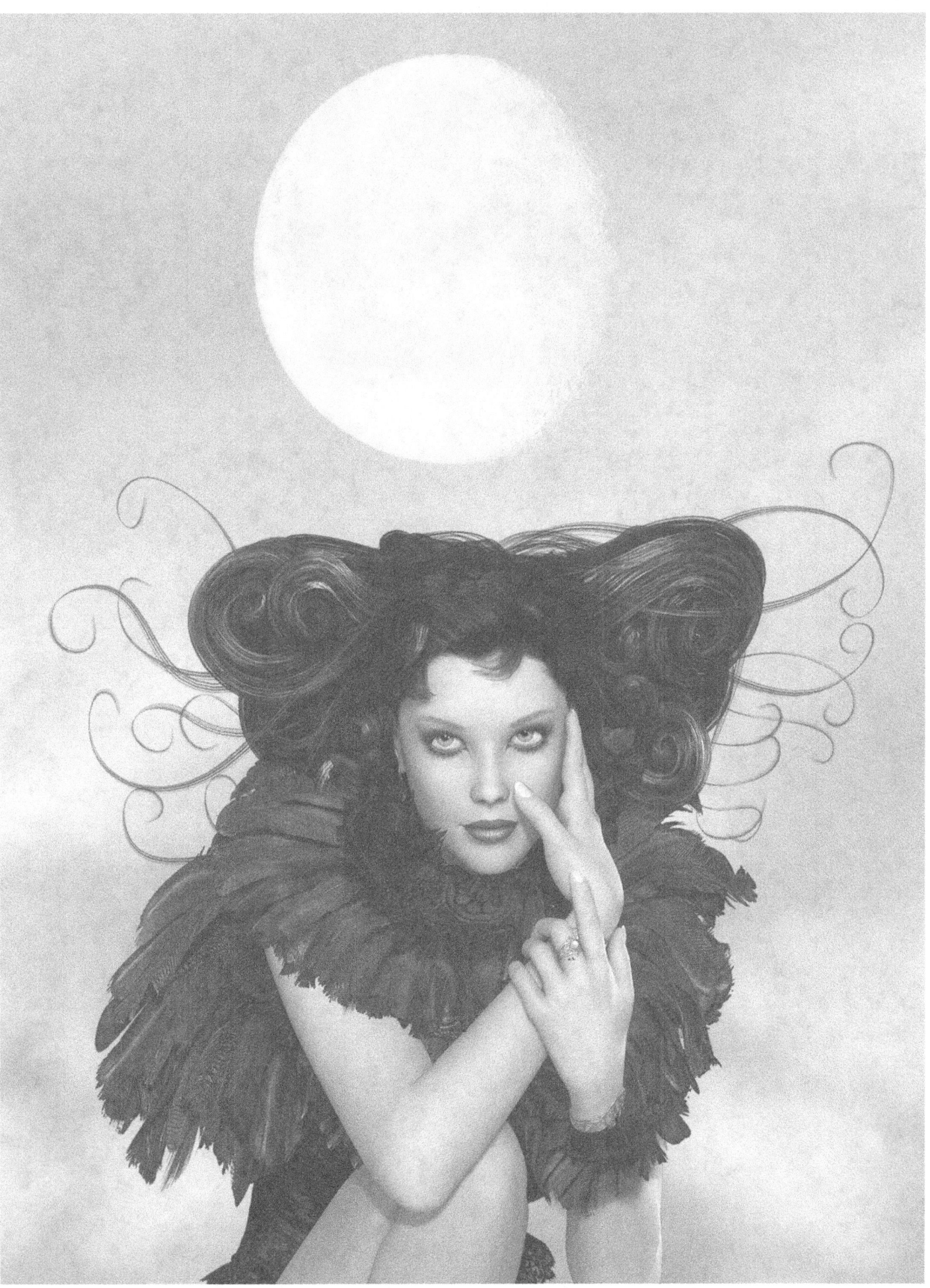

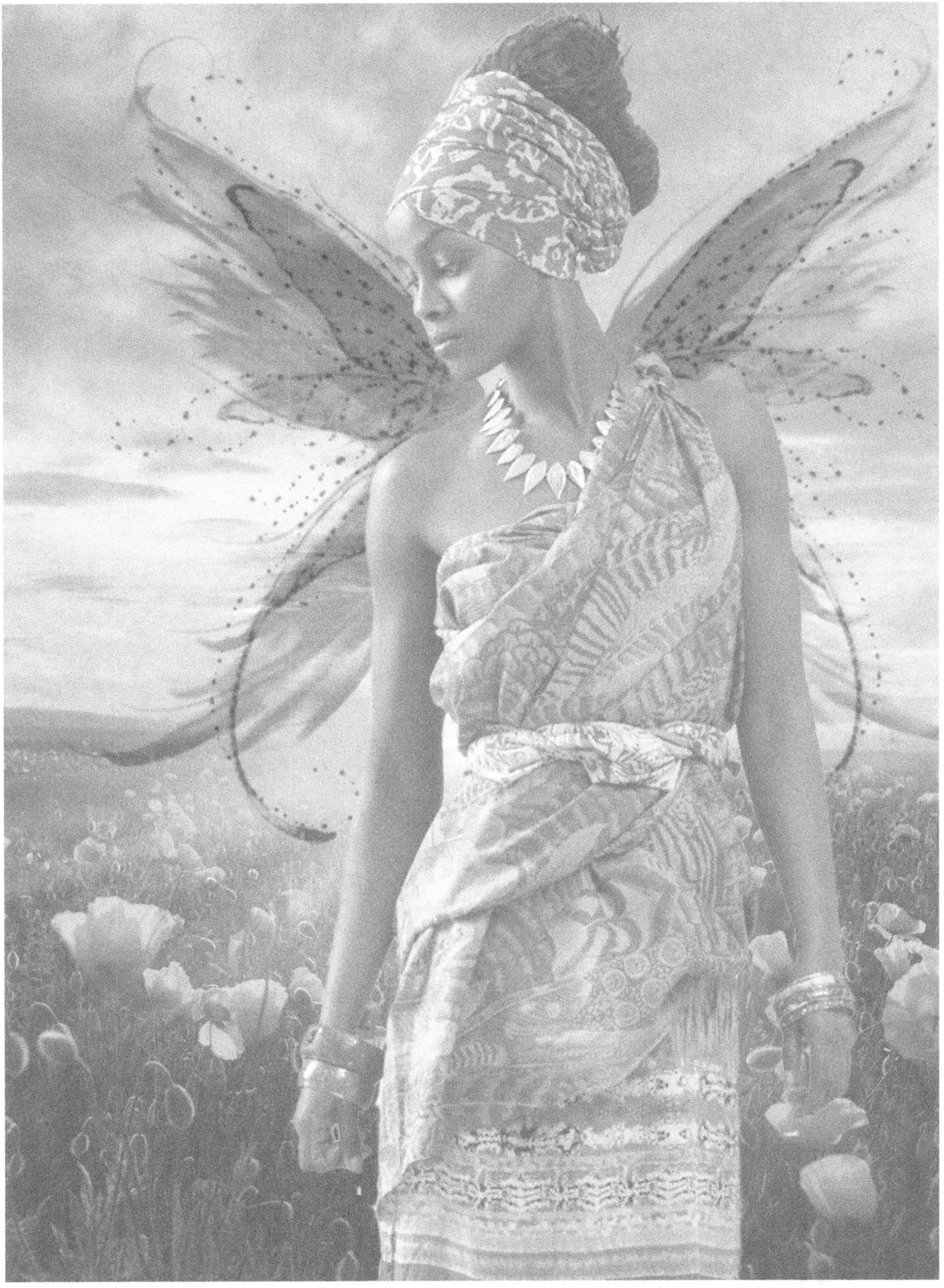

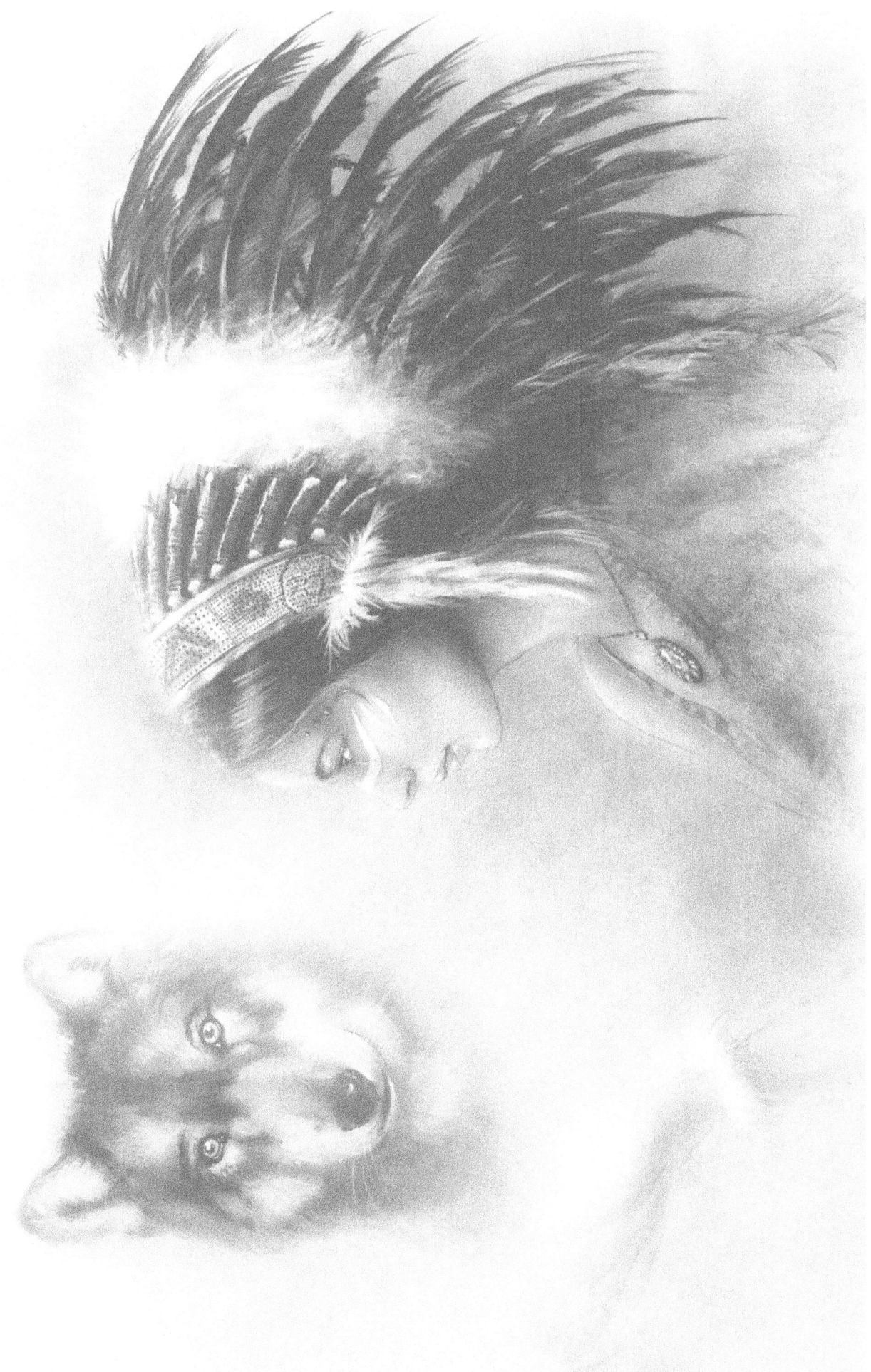

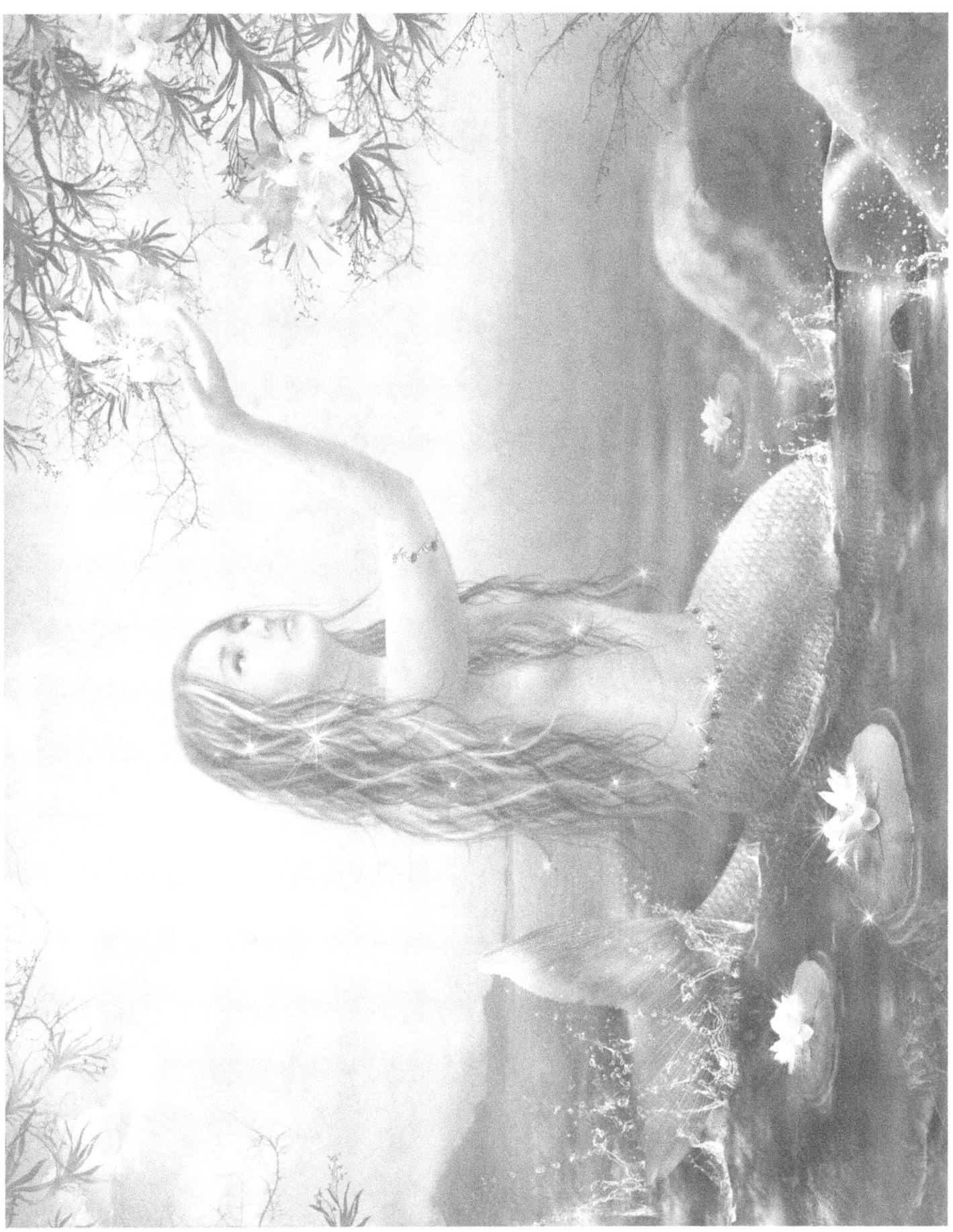

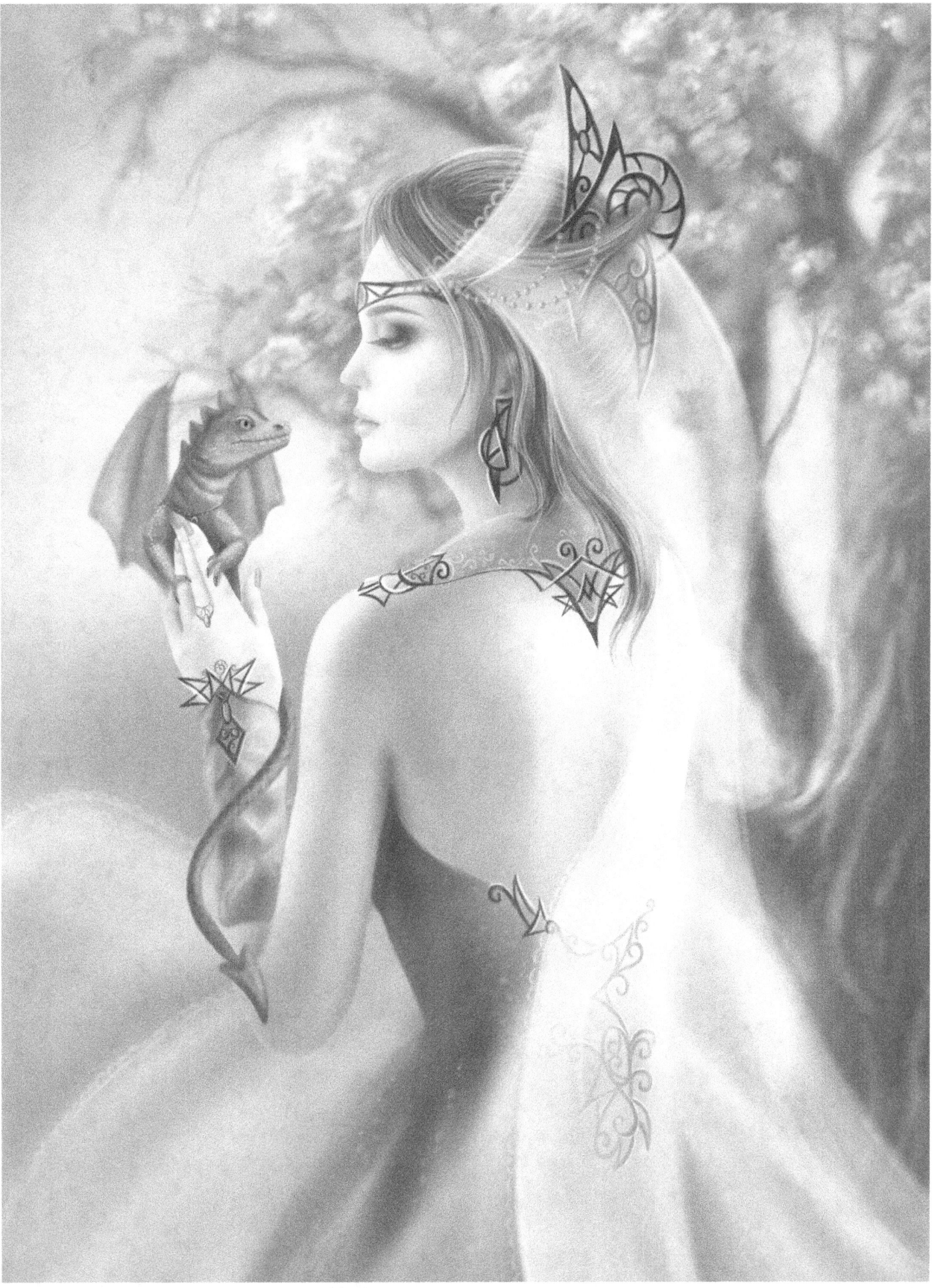

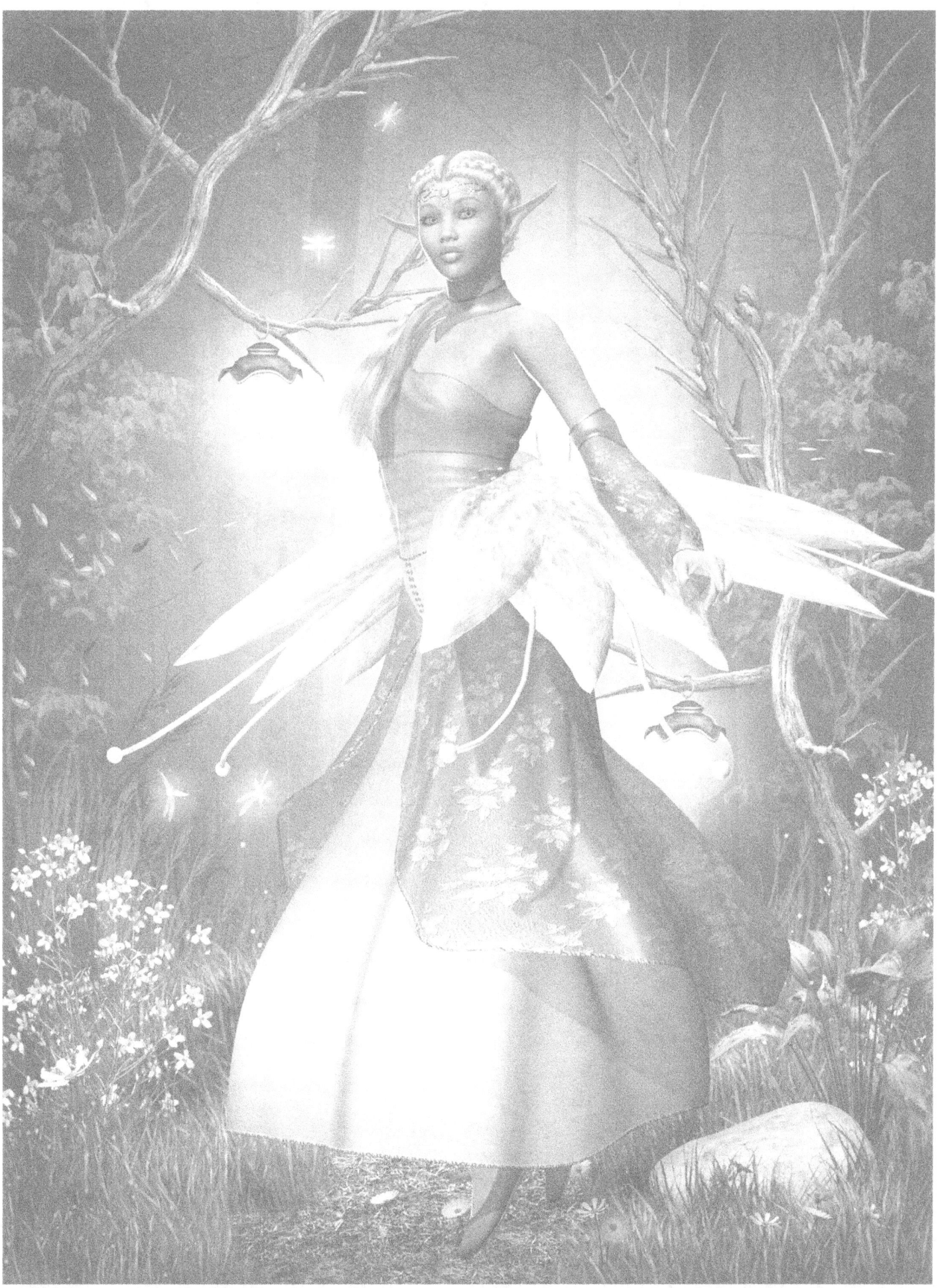

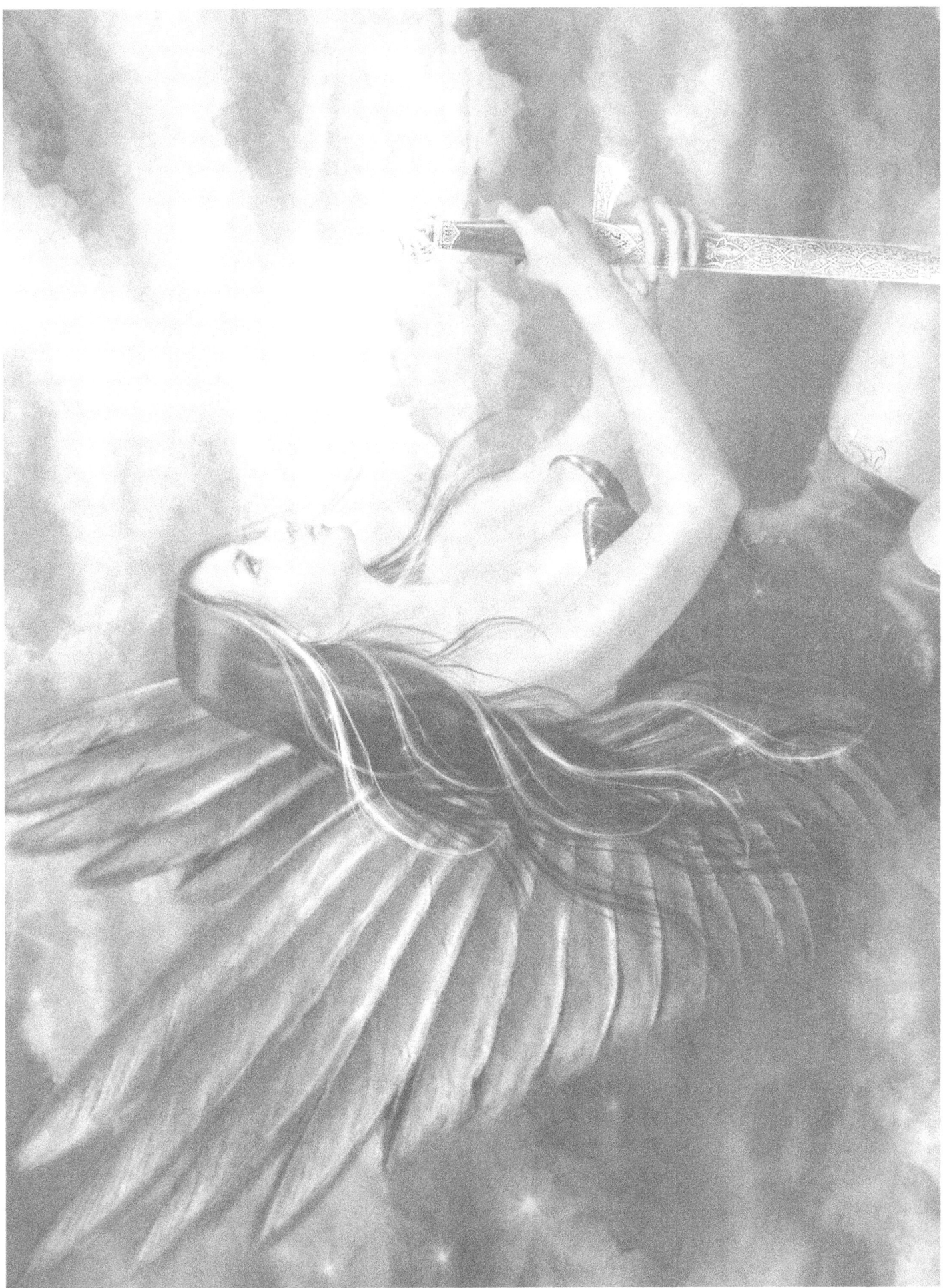

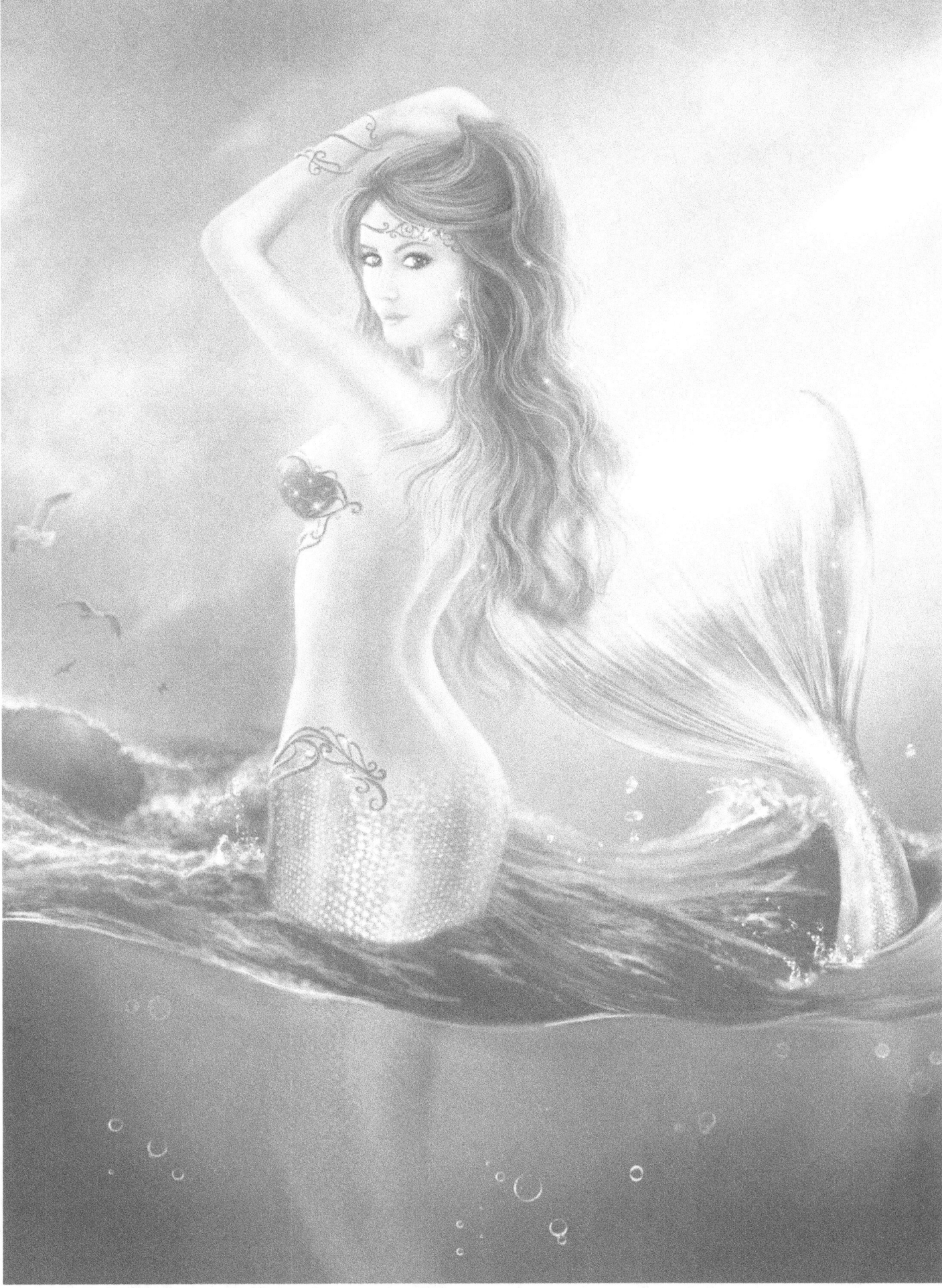

www.ingramcontent.com/pod-product-compliance
Lightning Source LLC
Chambersburg PA
CBHW080833180526
45168CB00006B/2668